DATE DUE

NEW DIRECTIONS
IN FAMILY THERAPY

NEW DIRECTIONS IN FAMILY THERAPY

Edited by

Timothy J. Buckley

John J. McCarthy

Elaine Norman

Mary Ann Quaranta

Distributed by:

DABOR SCIENCE PUBLICATIONS
Oceanside, New York 11572

Library of Congress Cataloging in Publication Data

Main entry under title:

New directions in family therapy.

   1. Family psychotherapy. I. Buckley,
Timothy J.
RC488.5.N5   616.8'915   77-22040
ISBN 0-89561-001-9

A Herbert Poster Book

Printed in the United States of America

TABLE OF CONTENTS

FOREWORD

This book addresses itself to some of the theoretical and practical aspects of family treatment at its present stage of development. All of the contributions were originally presented at an institute entitled "New Directions in Family Therapy," held at Fordham University, Lincoln Center.

The initial offering is by Salvador Minuchin, who is pre-eminent in the field of family treatment. To many, he is the quintessence of the family treatment movement. "Constructing A Therapeutic Reality," which was written after the publication of his most recent book, represents a further refinement of the conceptualization of family therapy.

Each of Dr. Minuchin's works is a clear and real advance over his previous formulations. "Family treatment," he states, "has come to a point of development at which it may be profitable for its practitioners to make their philosophies explicit. This paper has been written in this spirit." Minuchin claims no revolutionary conceptualization but offers us additional insight into the techniques which he has developed for advancing a productive and satisfactory reality for families who are experiencing difficulty. Dr. Minuchin does not believe that family treatment provides a tool for humanistic revolution, but effective work with a family can represent for that family a humanistic revolution in its own functioning.

The theoretical aspects of family treatment receive further consideration in Part II of this volume through contributions by Timothy Buckley, Ed Leonhard, and Lynn Hoffman. Professor Buckley's paper, "Commonalities and Differences in Theories and Techniques of Family Therapy," offers substantial aid to theoreticians, educators, and practitioners who are currently faced with a tremendous number of materials being published in the field, to say nothing of the number of training programs being established throughout the country. Although some do not agree with Professor Buckley's position that merely a "sectarian split" keeps us from a unified theory of family therapy, he offers a thorough review of the historical and contemporary developments in the family therapy movement. His contribution should be of particular interest to students of family therapy as they struggle with the similarities and differences among the various theories and approaches.

Dr. Leonhard's presentation seems to represent a natural outgrowth of Professor Buckley's position which accents similarities over differences. Dr. Leonhard presents his conceptualization and apparent comfort in practicing and teaching psychoanalysis and family therapy. His contribution, "Toward a New Formulation of Object Relation-Systems Theory from Analysis and Family Ecology Theories," cautions that he is not simply synthesizing two theories but that, in fact, he is articulating a new theory. There is no question that Dr. Leonhard breaks new conceptual ground which needs to be examined and studied carefully.

Ms. Lynn Hoffman's contribution, "Breaking the Homeostatic Cycle," discusses a search for a more economic and humane way of helping families where symptoms of dysfunction appear. She suggests an approach which involves ascertaining the variable that is being maintained, isolating the part played in it by the symptom, and then searching out the best way to block or stop the cycle from recurring. The goal is to accomplish this task in the most economic manner, and Ms. Hoffman attempts to identify some of the ways in which this may be achieved.

With the practical value of theoretical assumptions being the ultimate concern for those desiring to help families, Part III of this volume appropriately discusses special areas. Ms. Celia Dulvano's contribution, "Alcoholism in the Family System," is of particular importance to the many clinicians addressing therapeutic attention to the individual alcoholic. (There are an estimated nine million alcoholics in this country.) Ms. Dulvano helps us to understand some of the dynamics common to families with an alcoholic member; her case examples provide particularly valuable illustrations of these common patterns.

The findings reported by Drs. Flinn and Brown in "Opening Moves in Crisis Intervention with Families of Chronic Psychotics," refer to the growing use of the family as the unit of attention in work with psychotics, particularly with schizophrenics. As with the alcoholic patient, there is considerable evidence that more effective intervention is possible when the environment of the patient is the focus of therapy. Particularly helpful is Flinn and Brown's articulation of some specific principles which underline strategies for intervention with such families.

Working with the adolescent represents a great challenge to all in the helping professions. In Father John McCarthy's essay, he examines "The Resolution of the Adolescent Paradox through Family Treatment." In the absence of consensus among family therapists regarding the use of family therapy with adolescents, Fr. McCarthy spells out the indications and contra-indications for use of this approach with adolescents. My own contribution, "The Family Group Approach with Families of Children in Placement," attempts a beginning examination of the advantages of using this modality for the troubled families whose children need care outside their own homes.

A few specific issues are addressed in Part IV by Drs. Norman and Olds. Dr. Norman considers the impact of "Changing Sex Roles in Family Therapy" with the underlying assumption that some of the pathology found in troubled families is very much related to the sex role ideology of our country. Dr. Norman goes on to review some of the issues inherent in this assumption. The issue which Dr. Olds addresses is of a different order, that is, the use of "Co-therapists in Family Treatment." This essay reviews some of the advantages and disadvantages of co-therapy, with Dr. Olds' position leaning toward favoring co-therapy where this is feasible.

Special recognition must go to Professor Timothy Buckley and Father John McCarthy, S.J., for their editing and for the administrative work involved in this publication.

Mary Ann Quaranta, Dean
Graduate School of Social Service
Fordham University
Lincoln Center, New York

ACKNOWLEDGMENTS

Our efforts in the substantive aspects of the institute and in the publication of this volume would not have been possible without the expertise of the Office of Continuing Education of Fordham University under the leadership of Dr. Gary Fellows, assisted effectively by Ms. Denise Karikas. The editors were very fortunate to receive the generous assistance of Ms. Virginia Seymour in the clerical tasks and organization of the manuscript.

Although this work reflects the special interest of the faculty of the Fordham University Graduate School of Social Service, a special acknowledgment of appreciation is owed to Dr. Gilda Petraglia, Chair-person of the Micro Practice Sequence, and Professor Helen Dermody, then acting Dean of the School.

The Editors

PART ONE

STRUCTURAL APPROACH TO FAMILY THERAPY

CONSTRUCTING A THERAPEUTIC REALITY

Salvador Minuchin

Psychotherapy has been handicapped by the nineteenth century concept of man as a hero. Individual psychotherapy emphasizes psychological constructs inside the individual and elaborates counterpointal relationships between the individual and his context. This concept of the patient as a carrier of his psyche surrounded by the boundary of his skin required in complimentation the figure of therapist as an objective observer. The relationship between the therapist and the patient is organized according to rules that maintain both the therapist and the patient in parallel orbits while developing in fantasy transferential intimacy.

Pathology inside of the patient is related to fixation or dysfunctional learning at some point in early life. In all therapies, there is the assumption that it is essential to correct the early dysfunctional period in order to produce growth and change.

This has created an orientation in therapy that is the search for psychopathological dynamics. We have created a generation of sleuths who are looking for psychodynamic clues to the emotional crime. A generation of psychopathologists has been schooled in the search for the weakness in people's experience. This group of experts is objective, benevolent, and optimistic. They are clear that they are only explorers of the subterranean rivers which exist, that they are not adding to, or subtracting from, life. Therefore, they are not responsible for change, only for discovery.

Family therapy operates with the theoretical assumption that man is part of his context and that individual changes require a change in the reciprocal relationship of man in his context. Family therapy searches for pathology in the loop between the individual and his social network. The therapist joins the family in the therapeutic system and becomes part of the circumstances of the family members; as such, he intervenes, modifying the family members' experience and organizing and constructing their own reality.

This concept is troublesome because it means that a family's reality in therapy is a therapeutic construct. We have comfortably detoured around it in theoretical analysis of therapy by adhering to the concept of insight, so the therapist's task can be seen as merely exploration of the truth. The concept of therapeutic reality puts a heavy responsibility on the therapist: he must recognize that his input organizes the field of intervention and changes the family's reality and his own. The freedom of the therapist as a constructor of reality is limited by the finite reality of family structures in general and by the idiosyncratic way in which they are manifested in the patient's family.

With this conceptualization of therapy, it is essential to make explicit our map of normal family functioning as well as our ideas of therapeutic change.

CONCEPTS OF THE FAMILY

THE MATRIX OF IDENTITY

Family therapy is a product of the twentieth century philosophies that approach human beings as members of social groups which govern their behavior. This is a departure from the reification which has handicapped individual dynamic therapy, which puts the whole of the individual's life inside him, as though man remained constant in spite of his circumstances. In fact, family therapy has gone too close to the opposite pole, sometimes approaching the human being as a mere responder to field pressures.

Effective therapeutic techniques depend on a broad view of the human experience. It is perfectly correct to locate people's behavior in the feedback loops of social group processes, but it is important also to recognize that the individual has a range of responses to these processes. Within the family transactions, each family member has a number of choices. The wider his range of choice, the greater his experience of freedom within the system. This experience of freedom, or autonomy, is essential for the individual. Equally essential is a sense of belonging—of coming from a certain reference group. Indeed, the individual's sense of well-being depends on the proportioning of these two ingredients; dependency and autonomy are complementary, not conflicting characteristics of the human condition. Their proportioning is negotiated in the development of the system and crystallized by the current social context.

Families mold and program the child's sense of identity early in the socialization process. The sense of belonging comes with the child's accommodation to the groups within the family and with his assumption of the transactional patterns which form the family structure. The sense of autonomy occurs through participation in different family subsystems in different contexts as well as through participation in extrafamilial groups. A psychological and transactional territory is carved out for each person, a territory which is determined by the contrapuntal relationships of individual and system.

The family, then, is the matrix of its members' sense of identity—of belonging and of being different. Its chief task is to foster their psychosocial growth and well-being throughout their life in common. This is the first element of a family therapist's schema of a family.

The family also forms the smallest social unit which transmits a society's demands and values, and thus, preserves them. The family therapist, therefore, must see the family as the link between the individual and larger social units. The family must adapt to society's needs while it fosters its members' growth, all the while maintaining enough continuity to fulfill its function as the individual's reference group.

THE FAMILY AS A SYSTEM

The family therapist must also recognize that the human family is a social system which operates through transactional patterns. These are repeated interactions which establish patterns of how, when, and to whom to relate. When a mother tells her child to drink his juice and he obeys, this interaction defines who she is in relation to him and who he is in relation to her in that context and at that time. Repeated operations build patterns, and these patterns underpin the family system. The patterns which evolve become familiar and preferred. The system maintains itself within a preferred range, and deviations which pass the system's threshold of tolerance usually elicit counterdeviation mechanisms which reestablish the accustomed range.

THE SYSTEM DEVELOPS OVER TIME

In his early development within the specificity of his family context, the child develops certain parts of his biopsychological potential, and this is what he becomes familiar with as being himself. In the measure in which the child encounters other social groups and develops in another context new areas of competence and interpersonal skill, certain aspects of his personality are activated in his complementary relationships with significant people. The potential of the individual becomes developed and restricted at the same time as certain types of transactions become more available and familiar. These responses tend to be identified as self while other aspects of self remain potentially available and some hardly available by disuse.

A reciprocal interplay develops by which the individual determines the range of his responses. Certain aspects of his personality are confirmed more frequently by significant people as self, and that reinforces the continuous use of certain alternative behavior and modalities of being.

When people marry, they must develop a number of common transactional patterns. Each spouse has his own behavior pattern and value system, including expectations of how people should and will relate to him. These patterns clash and mesh in the small events of daily life, and each spouse changes in accommodation to the other.

Areas of autonomy and complementarity are defined. The range of choices narrows, and after some period of life together, the range is reduced to the preferred patterns. The spouses become predictable to each other. In areas of narrowed experiential range, the spouses develop implicit or explicit contracts with value overtones. Even dysfunctional patterns can become preferred, and the couple will maintain them as long as possible. If the patterns are violated, each spouse may feel betrayed though neither may remember the origin of the pattern.

But family circumstances change through time, and the family must be able to change. Other transactional patterns are activated, and new structures develop in a balanced process of morphostasis and morphogenesis. Alternative transactional patterns always exist within a system though these are hidden from the observer by the dominant preferred patterns. But when change becomes necessary, the functional family activates the alternative patterns of the system.

THE DIFFERENTIATION OF THE SYSTEM

Family systems are differentiated; they carry out tasks through subsystems. Individuals are subsystems within a family (as are dyads like husband and wife and larger subgroupings formed by generation, by gender, or by tasks). People accommodate kaleidoscopically in different subsystems to achieve the mutuality necessary for human intercourse. A child has to act like a son so his father can act like a father, but he may take on executive powers when he is alone with his younger brother.

The rules defining who participates within a subsystem, and how, are the subsystem boundaries. The functioning of these boundaries is an important key to the system's viability. They must be defined well enough to allow subsystem members to carry out their functions, but they must not isolate the subsystem from the rest of the system.

The nuclear family has at least three subsystems—spouse, parental, and sibling. These subsystems are units with differentiated functions. They offer and demand the exercise of specific social skills in different contexts. In the parental or executive subsystem, for example, parents and children negotiate decisions from positions of unequal power. In the sibling subsystem, children interact more as peers, negotiating issues of competition, defeat, accommodation, cooperation, and protection. The spouse subsystem is an arena of complementarity—of learning how to give in without the feeling that one has given up.

Each subsystem must keep negotiating boundaries which protect it from interference so that it can fulfill its functions and resolve its problems. But the boundaries' selective permeability does not preclude the possibility of summoning other family members to resolve specific subsystem problems.

The family is a differentiated social unit structured by transactional patterns. In some areas, the system is quite flexible, offering a broad range of choices. In other areas, preferred patterns are tightly maintained. Alternative patterns exist but are not used. The family is constantly subjected to demands for change sparked by developmental changes in its own members and by extrafamilial pressures. Responding to these demands from within and without requires transformation. The positions of family members *vis-à-vis* each other and the external world change and *must* change. But the system must also maintain the continuity to protect its members' sense of belonging.

Stresses are inherent. All families are subject to crises when a member enters a new developmental stage, or a new member joins, a former member leaves, or when the family is making contact with social institutions, etc. In general, families respond to these periods of existential crisis by marshalling their resources. If necessary, alternative transactional patterns are mobilized, and there evolve new ways of responding to change of circumstances.

FAMILY PATHOLOGY

Sometimes, some families respond to demands for change by increasing the rigidity of their preferred transactional patterns. The range of choices narrows, and family members develop stereotyped responses to each other and to the extrafamilial. The family becomes a closed system, and family members experience themselves as controlled and impotent. At this point, a family comes to therapy. Often, the stereotyping process has led to labeling one family member the deviant. Or the family may enter therapy because of "lack of communication" or "inability to cope."

Difficulties in a family are not an indicator for therapeutic restructuring. The difficulties of performing a family's tasks in modern society are real and intense, and stress in a family system is anything but abnormal. Family therapists may minimize the real problems inherent in the processes of adapting while maintaining continuity, just as individual dynamic therapists have minimized the difficulties in the individual's social context. A family in transition should not be labeled pathological. That label should be reserved for families who increase the rigidity of their transactional patterns in the face of stress, avoiding or resisting any exploration of alternatives.

For example, a couple in therapy began seriously to contemplate divorce when the husband's union was engaged in a bitter strike. The husband's position was "You refuse to take my needs into consideration. You have always exploited me because of my sense of responsibility and duty. I will not give in to you any longer. I have begun to realize that I have rights, and my dignity as a human being is paramount." The wife's position was "You are selfish. You have stopped considering the family's needs and are concerned only with your own. You are so wrapped up in yourself that you don't see me. If you want to leave, you can go now instead of asking me to do things for you like a typical male chauvinist." The therapist read the decision to consider divorce as the effect of massive intrusion of the extrafamilial context in spouse conflicts, which was resulting in increased stereotyping. He strongly advised them not to come to any decision until the strike was over, and he pointed out to the couple how much the husband's position resembled his union's stance in the strike negotiations and how much the wife sounded like the management. Two weeks after the settlement of the strike, the couple wanted to stay together and work on the problems of the family.

THE FAMILY IN THERAPY

The family therapist's definition of a pathogenic family, then, is a family whose adaptive and coping mechanisms have been exhausted. Family members are chronically trapped in stereotyped patterns of interaction which are severely limiting their range of choice, but no alternatives seem possible. In this time of heightened rigidity of transactional patterns, conflict overshadows large areas of normal functioning. Often, one family member is the identified patient, and the other family members see themselves as accommodating to his illness. The family has gone through a reification process which gives priority to dysfunctional areas.

In most cases, it is not essential to explore the development of these dysfunctional patterns. The family's history is manifest in the present, and change can be achieved only in the present. It is possible to explore any family member's past or open up alternative modalities of being with the family of origin, but it is not necessary. The exploration of the hows of our previous relationships can be significant in understanding how we became what we are, but it is usually not necessary for changing the present family context. The therapeutic process will be the process of changing family members' psychosocial positions vis-à-vis each other. The therapist may or may not try to help his patients understand their narrowed reality. But he will always address himself to the actualization of possible change. He may tell a family member that he is dependent, or angry, or depressed. But he will know that this focus can reinforce the already crystallized interactions. He may or may not explore the family members' feelings, but he will always explore the system of mutual complementarity that elicits those feelings. This approach emphasizes the transactional nature of experience and simultaneously suggests the possibility of change.

Of course, any description of therapeutic technique presupposes that the therapist has begun to join the family in such a way that family members trust him even if they do not agree with him. The therapist must know how to affiliate with the family and support them through the sense of dislocation which they will experience as change develops.

CHALLENGING THE PATIENT'S REALITY

The first step in the process of change is a challenge to family members' self-perception and experience of reality. Challenging reality is a prerequisite for change common to all therapeutic processes. In psychoanalysis, the analyst challenges the patient's experience of reality on the basis of an expanded self. The patient is taught that the psychological life is larger than the conscious experience, and he learns to free-associate in order to block the usual screening processes with which he organizes his reality. The analyst organizes the data which the patient presents according to psychoanalytic constructions.

In family therapy, the challenge is based on the axiom that family members have alternative ways of transacting. The family therapist does not challenge his patients, only their patterns of interaction. What we call reality is the reality of the most preferred or available experiences. The purpose of therapy is to activate certain aspects of the individual and the system which render available new modalities of transaction. In a family where the husband was overly central, for example, the therapist paid special attention to the wife's feeble efforts to communicate, conveying the impression that her inputs were more meaningful than her husband's. In a family whose identified patient was a college dropout who had been diagnosed as schizophrenic, the therapist supported the mother, who was willing to consider her son lazy, and snubbed the father, a very competent physician who preferred a "crazy" son to a failure. In other words, the therapist joins the family in ways that make it possible to activate the alternatives whose presence he postulates.

A family with an identified patient has gone through a reification process which overfocuses on one member; the therapist reverses this process. He enters and joins the family by paying attention to the family-evolved reality—the symptoms of the identified patient. He then expands his focus to the symptom-bearer and then abandons the symptom-bearer in order to move toward family interaction. This sequence may occur in the first session, or it may develop over a number of sessions. For example, in a family with a bright seventeen-year-old boy who was failing in school, the parents and a younger sibling spent much of the first session discussing the identified patient's school performance. He remained silent, acting uncomfortable when attacked but for the most part, lost in his own thoughts. The mother said to the father that if the boy went to a private school where he could be challenged, his performance might improve. The father said that this was unrealistic, for it would involve great financial sacrifice for the whole family. He added that the mother was blind to the boy's laziness. Finally, he said that if the boy did go to private school, it would have to be her responsibility. But if she wanted to deprive the whole family, he would consent.

The therapist talked with the identified patient about his school, his friends, his areas of difficulty and interest, his teachers, and his plans for next year. He challenged him for letting his parents make such an important decision for him. He suggested that the boy was acting like an eleven year old; only thus was it appropriate for his younger brother to discuss him with his parents while he remained silent. He also pointed out that the boy was manipulating his parents to control him by acting younger than he was. Then, the therapist challenged the parents for taking decision-making power away from the boy. He then moved away from the identified patient to the parents and explored the coalition between mother and son that left father feeling excluded. The mother's plight came into focus: how the family made her the center for decisions, overburdening her, and how her own orientation toward serving her family facilitated this overcentralization.

The third session was held with husband and wife alone. The focus went back to the older boy's problems in school, but now the utilization of these problems in the family was very much part of the picture.

The speed of the movement from symptom to patient to family will depend on the nature and intensity of the symptom, the flexibility of family interaction, and the therapist's style. When a symptom is serious, the family system is extremely rigid. In such a case, the therapist must stay with the symptom of the identified patient for a while. Moving away from it will increase the pressure within the system, increasing the symptom's intensity until the therapist responds to the family's reality. When the identified patient's symptoms are milder, the therapist can move faster.

PSYCHOTHERAPY AS AN EXPERIMENTAL FIELD

How does the therapist become acquainted with a family's range of possible interactions, challenge the present straitened reality, create the possibilities for alternative interactions, and still support family members and maintain himself in a position of expert leadership? This is the artistry of therapy, no doubt. But it is buttressed by the therapist's map of his goals and by the planned flexibility of the experimenter.

The therapist meets a field of stabilized family interactions. He becomes involved with the family members while observing how they interact. He tracks the content of their communications and the ways they communicate. He tests the limits of family flexibility, requesting the family members to interact in a different way.

He lets himself be organized by the family's response to his inputs. This way, his inputs can challenge family interactions without going beyond the thresholds which the system can tolerate. When he suggests a modification of the way family members interact, he is introducing an experimental probe. The responses will give him information about unmapped areas and directions for his next intervention. Some discussions of therapeutic strategies make it seem that the therapist's strategies are organized regardless of the family's feedback. In the reality of therapy, however, family responses modify the therapist's behavior, and the therapist must be alert to these responses to confirm his hunches or change his strategies.

For example, a newly married couple with a twelve-year-old child from the wife's previous marriage came to therapy because of the child's crippling asthma. He had had asthma since the age of two and had always slept with his mother. With the mother's remarriage, his asthmatic attacks had increased, especially at night. He now had his own room, but usually his mother or stepfather slept in his room to allay his fear and monitor his wheezing. The therapist directed the parents to shut the door of their bedroom, not to go to the child's bedroom unless it was absolutely necessary, and never to sleep with him. He discussed the fact that the family was in a transitional situation, and everyone would have to adapt to the new circumstances. The task was unsuccessful. The mother was convinced of the necessity for change, but she was unable to ignore her son's calling her for fear of precipitating a serious attack. The therapist learned that this route to change was closed.

In the next session, he asked the boy for the names of two close friends at school. The boy, a loner, took almost three minutes to give two names. The mother tried hard to attract his attention so she could prompt him, but the boy, acting on a suggestion the therapist had made earlier, did not look at her. The therapist got up from his chair to give the boy a handshake. He labeled the three minutes' thinking for himself a triumph of autonomy and discussed how difficult the task was for the mother. He further discussed with the boy and stepfather what kinds of things they could do to block respectfully mother's unnecessary interventions. An exploratory task had indicated a closed pathway. Another had indicated a new and promising direction.

CONSTRUCTING THE THERAPEUTIC REALITY

A therapist never deals with a family's whole reality. He never knows the dynamics of the total situation, and he begins his therapeutic challenge before he has learned a great deal about the family. The only purpose of the beginning interventions is to shake the rigidity of the field. If the alternatives the therapist indicates feel right to the family members on some level, the processed change has begun. But even when the therapist and family are well into the therapeutic process, the therapist is operating in terms of partial constructs. His position in the therapeutic system organizes his own reality and programs his experience of the patients' reality. Second, the therapist will dismiss many elements of the family's life as "not part of the therapeutic reality." In effect, the therapist selects partial constructs to be the reality of therapy, in accordance with his goals.

To change the reality of a patient, we need to change the reality of the relationship between the patient and his context. The therapist finds himself in the position of a "constrained changer." The family has the capacity to control him by determining his complimentary responses. The family also may activate his rescue fantasy and induct him into supplementing the system's needs. The therapist, then, is in and out of a system that he has the task to change. He can operate as an active participant transacting with family members, part of a dyad or triad, or as a creator and director of family scenarios; in both situations he will facilitate the experiencing of alternative reality. In every situation, he has the limitation of his own life experience, his value system, and his esthetic sense. Nonetheless, paradoxically, the more real the therapist's involvement is, the more objective and experimental he becomes.

Sometimes, the therapist is simply picking one point in a circle and calling it the beginning. For example, a man and woman who have been married for twenty years are discussing their sex life. For as long as they can remember, they have agreed that the wife should close the door when she wants sex. The husband is unhappy about this because he feels that he should initiate the act. The wife claims he *does* initiate; she closes the door when she sees that he wants sex. The husband says that she initiates it: whenever the wife looks at him in ways that indicate she is wondering if he wants sex, he indicates that he does. The feedback process can be elaborated further and further back. The therapist picks any point of entry that seems promising.

But a therapeutic construct can also be a new causal linking for the family, one which allows them to reorient their positions *vis-à-vis* each other. For example, in a session a younger sister attacked her older sister, the identified patient, aged thirteen by deriding her for letting their stepfather bathe her. The therapist challenged the mother for "allowing her daughter to tattle about family situations." The actual event was that the younger daughter talked and the mother was silent. The therapist's construction, "You allowed her to talk," connected two events in a statement of causality which shifted the mother's anger, which for the first time, was directed at the younger daughter instead of the older girl.

A young husband described a situation in which he had been very depressed. He said that his wife suggested that she return to her parents in order to protect him in this situation. The wife had transformed an event in her husband's life to an interspouse problem. The therapist went one step farther and challenged the ease of the wife's move from wife to daughter, including the extended family in a therapeutic construct.

The father of a fourteen-year-old educable retarded child picked up a ball which the boy had dropped and put it in his lap. Later in the session, the boy dropped the ball again, and this time, the therapist put it in his lap. Clearly, he had been inducted by the family's organization around the boy, which had rendered this child almost helpless. If the therapist had instead challenged the parents for immobilizing the boy, the slender event could have generated sufficient emotional intensity to further therapeutic change.

The first session with a family with an anorectic daughter finished with the whole family experiencing the child as protecting her mother from the loneliness of her relationship with her busy, aloof husband. The anorexia at the center of the family's life receded, to be replaced by the therapeutically highlighted distance between the spouses.

A FAMILY THERAPY GRAMMAR

With this view of family therapy as a construction of reality, it is useful to derive certain *ad hoc* rules which form an intermediate step between the basic steps of therapy and the therapeutic reality. Rules can help an inexperienced therapist operate with some level of competence while he still feels ignorant. They can, also, direct an experienced therapist through the beginning stages of therapy with a family he doesn't yet know.

The rules discussed below are instructions which I find myself repeating to different therapists who treat families. They have a certain universality because they spring from generic ideas about the family and the therapeutic process, but they are rules only in the sense of something that is repeated. They will probably be correct about sixty percent of the time; that is, they are better than chance. But their usefulness diminishes as the idiosyncracies of each therapeutic system appear.

CREATING THE THERAPEUTIC SYSTEM

The therapist must establish himself as the leader of the therapeutic unit; this is a *sine qua non* of therapy. To assume leadership, he needs to join the family, accommodating himself to its transactional patterns. This process of joining is essential before and at the time that the therapist introduces restructuring maneuvers.

His restructuring interventions are directed toward making alternative transactions available. He directs the family to explore these alternatives by entering into alliances and coalitions with different family members. In these processes, the therapist moves from a position of proximity, in which he interacts with other members of the therapeutic system, to a disengaged position from which he directs family members to enact certain transactions, creating interpersonal scenarios which become the experiential field of the family member.

Some family therapists suggest that the therapist must be indirect in his goals because family members will resist direct leadership. While this position is sometimes correct, it is frequently unnecessary. When properly joined by the therapist, family members cooperate with him in the therapeutic process. When the therapist is enabling, his inputs will not be resisted.

The therapist organizes the process in terms of what is possible. If a diagnosis creates a solution that does not help, the "beginning of the circle" can be set at another point. The therapist will construct the truths of therapy according to what is most possible and least painful for the family. Every technique/strategy is measured only insofar as it is goal-related. These strategies are good or bad because of how they work, not right or wrong on some truth scale. Being correct has nothing to do with relevance. The therapist must learn to focus on that which is relevant: "truth" needs to be relevant.

SUPPORTING THE FAMILY'S FUNCTIONS

Other middle range concepts of therapy can be derived from concepts of normal family dynamics. The family system supports individuation and differentiation. It supports, also, a sense of belonging. The therapist must support both.

RULES THAT SUPPORT INDIVIDUATION

Family members should speak for themselves. They should tell their own story. Family members should not tell what other members think or feel although they should be encouraged to ask the speaker questions. Two members should not discuss a third member who is present without his participation. Family members should be discouraged from asking each other for data they should know or from consistently checking, verbally or nonverbally, for approval of statements or actions. Competent acts should be signaled whenever they occur, and family members should be encouraged to enact transactions competently.

Dealing with an identified patient, the therapist should avoid crystallizing the symptoms by discussing other positive and negative aspect of the symptom-bearer and of other family members. Broadening the focus to the complementary underpinnings of the symptom—who elicits it, what its function is—also is helpful. If two members of the family have labeled a third the deviant, the therapist should not address himself to the identified patient immediately. He should go to another family member to try to elicit different data, so the identified patient does not experience the therapist as joining in the process of labeling him. However, the therapist will usually avoid joining with the scapegoated family member against the other family members because of the danger that the more powerful members will attack the therapist through his vulnerable ally and intensify the scapegoating. The therapist determines the success of tasks because success is defined by the therapist's punctuation. The end of a transaction can be longer or shorter depending on the therapeutic goal.

RULES WHICH SUPPORT SYSTEM FUNCTIONING

The therapist often will work to clarify or reinforce functional subsystem boundaries. For example, he will almost automatically support the boundaries which define the executive subsystem. If the spouses elicit a child's support when discussing a husband-wife issue, this will be blocked. When spouses and therapist discuss a couple's sexual life, other family members should be asked to leave the room. It is preferable, if the identified patient is a child, not to enter the conflicts of husband and wife before the therapeutic system is established well enough for the family members to know that they can depend on the therapist. Spouse conflicts, in such cases, may appear early in therapy, but the therapist must not explore this area until he knows that the family trusts him to defend them.

The functions of each subsystem will be rewarded. If a member of a family is doing well, for example, the therapist can appreciate the other person's complementarity in facilitating the behavior. That is, parents may be complimented when their child improves.

When members of a subsystem are defined as unequal, the therapist may relabel the definition of power (for instance, saying to the supposed weak spouse, "How do you get your wife to organize your actions?"). The exploration of complementarity moves members away from accusation and stereotyping.

When working with a subsystem, the therapist may ask members who do not belong to that subsystem to leave the room or move their chairs back to define their noninvolvement.

The therapist can use subsystems to define problems or to change moods. If the adolescents of a large family are experiencing difficulty in negotiating issues of independence, separate sessions can be held with the parents and adolescents, with the younger children excluded. When working in a hostile atmosphere between spouses, the therapist can promote mood-change by bringing in the children, moving the spouse subsystem to the parental subsystem.

These are *ad hoc* rules to be discarded as each therapeutic system develops and its elements become clear.

Family therapy has come to a point of development at which it may be profitable for its practitioners to make their philosophies explicit; this paper has been written in this spirit. In conclusion, I would like to point out one thing which I think family therapy is not. It is *not* a tool for humanistic revolution. In fact, it is often the opposite: one of the family's tasks is to provide continuity with a society which the family therapist, in his own value system, may consider restrictive. Family therapy is the active process of changing dysfunctional patterns of transaction and eliciting available alternative patterns. It is a process in which therapist and family members work together searching and enacting an alternative reality that expands the possibility of the family and family members.

PART TWO

THEORETICAL EXPLORATIONS

INTRODUCTION

One of the most frequent questions posed to psychotherapists by new patients "in the know" is "to what school of psychotherapy or psychology do you belong?." This question is reflective of the most intellectually obstructing problem in the field of psychological or mental health science today. One needs to have only a cursory knowledge of the field to realize that it is cluttered with rival sectarian associations vying for the label of orthodoxy. These claims to the right (ortho) doctrine (doxy) have divided psychoanalysts into the Orthodox, the Neo-Freudians, the Existentialists (Daseinsanalyse), the Ego-Analysts, and the Kleinians (Object Relations), to mention only the better known schools. Beyond the pale of psychoanalysis, we sight myriad sects and splinter sects of psychotherapeutic belief, some organized around one single concept, while others have been excommunicated from the psychoanalytic affiliation for attempting to introduce deviationist thoughts. Among these factions, one finds the schools of Harry Stack Sullivan's "Interpersonal Relations Theory," Carl Roger's "Client Centered" Psychotherapy, Karen Horney's "Character Analysis," Joseph Wolpe's "Reciprocal Inhibition Psychotherapy"—the basis for B.F. Skinner's "Behavior Modification"—and Janov's "Primal Scream Therapy."

In their literature, the more secure and widely accepted schools of thought can choose to ignore the very existence of the other schools as they produce countless exegeses of the basic tenets of their school. The smaller and the more recently arrived groups, on the other hand, seem to feel the need to slay the giants in order to justify their respective existences. Some promote the rumor that psychoanalysis is dead or at least, no longer relevant; others strive to prevail upon us that the unconscious does not exist; some that the intrapsyche has no bearing on the interpersonal, and yet others that the interpersonal has no bearing on behavior. One more recent group would call down a pox on all these houses with

21

their insistence that only the socio-cultural-political milieu can explain human behavior.

The recent arrival of family therapy on the scene did little to promote any spirit of ecumenicity (belonging to the whole). As the obvious became undeniable, some therapists who had pledged sole allegiance to the intrapsychic etiology experienced great conflict upon recognizing the role of the family as a dynamic interactional unit in the production of pathological or dysfunctional behavior. The outcome was not an integration of the new finding into the already held theory but rather, a compulsion to make an either/or choice. The converts to the new ideology of family therapy frequently became the most zealous antagonists of psychotherapy with individuals and particularly with psychoanalysis.

Yet, family therapy itself was not to be spared the divisive development of its principal predecessor, psychoanalysis. In the first chapter of this section, Buckley attempts to identify those elements which unite all the schools of family therapy and the issues which drive them into factionalism. The basic proposition of his article is that each school or major theorist is, in fact, correct as is borne out by the results of their therapeutic intervention but correct only to a point. Like the parts of a jigsaw puzzle, they make greater sense when joined together correctly. The difficulty in joining some of the pieces together suggests that some of the interjacent pieces are missing. He proposes that the different emphasis of each school derives from the various points at which each one entered the field of family therapy. This is akin to the story of the group of blindfolded men given the task of describing an elephant by touch. In no way could one understand that each was describing the same object without being privy to the nature of the object. Buckley concludes his overview of the field of family therapy with an invitation not to an eclectic approach but to a holistic vision in which the whole is greater than the sum of its parts and within which the current diverse interventive methodologies would receive even greater approbation.

In the second paper of this section, Leonhard is concerned about the same basic issue as Buckley, especially with the needless warring betwee|r the proponents of intrapsychic and extrapsychic therapies. Being, like Buckley, both a psychoanalyst and a family therapist, Leonhard is interested in Freudian psychodynamic, Object Relations Theory (Fairbairn, Winicott, Guntrip, and Klein) and the non-linear Ecological (extrapsychic) causes of human behavior. To span the dichotomy perceived by the proponents of these two disparate theoretical concepts, he proposes a fascinating theory which unites the concepts inherent in both schools into a formulation which is greater than the mere sum of both parts. He calls his theory an "Object Relation-Systems Theory." In it, he combines two levels of human interaction, the intra-psychic world of interacting introjects and the extra-psychic world of interacting external objects, and concludes to a third system of interacting objects, viz. the interaction of introjected objects with external objects in various combinations. The ramifications of this theoretical conceptualization for the family therapy systems approach are phenomenal. Altering the real interactions of the family may not suffice to effect change in one or several members manifesting symptomatic behavior if such interactions are being perceived in combination with introjected objects. He describes the person-family unit as a configuration of mutually interacting system and subsystems which involves both the intra-psychic object relations world of each member as well as the extra-psychic world of interpersonal relations in a constant state of cybernetic interplay.

The third paper in this section, by Hoffman, like the previous two papers, is concerned with theoretical formulations but differs in that it is more narrowly focused on a specific conceptualization within the Structural Approach to family therapy. Her concern in working with a family with a problem is to determine what interactive processes in the family need to be the target of change. She posits that the symptomatic behavior of the child in a family is a part of the family's homeostatic system, and that behavior is maintained by a recurrent sequence of interactive moves involving diads or triads in the family. This repetitive pattern of interaction she calls a "cycle," which seems very similar to Minuchin's "dysfunctional set." In this paper, she gives vivid examples from actual cases, which leave no doubt as to what she means. She considers, also, the relation of the "cycle" to the closeness-distance needs of the family and how to intervene to break the cycle.

These three theoretical papers in no way begin to cover the full range of theoretical issues or considerations which grow out of this approach to psychotherapy. The purpose of this section is not to cover the full range of family therapy theory but rather, to draw the attention of family therapists, both seasoned and new, to the fact that theory *does* matter because how we look at the family is already determined by our theoretical frame of reference (as Hoffman clearly demonstrates). This return to a thoughtful scrutiny of our theoretical base is imperative, especially today when the emphasis of the literature is on technique.

COMMONALITIES AND DIFFERENCES IN THEORIES AND TECHNIQUES OF FAMILY THERAPY

Timothy J. Buckley

The "succès d'estime" which family therapy enjoys today represents one of the greatest achievements in the history of mental health. It is not more than twenty years ago that courageous individuals like Nathan Ackerman began to call on the mental health profession to look to the family for both the origin and the remedy of much of the human dysfunction classified under the rubric of mental illness. Today, training programs in family therapy abound not only in the traditional separate family therapy training centers but also, in schools of medicine psychoanalytic training centers, and schools of social work.

In 1972, an analysis of the literature conducted by Alan Gurman, Ph.D., revealed that family therapy experienced the onset of its "major growth spurt" after 1960, with roughly half of the publications appearing since 1967. The widespread acceptance of family therapy was reflected in Gurman's finding that the "journals contributing the most to the development of marital therapy form a heterogeneous mixture of professional disciplines, with multidisciplinary journals demonstrating the greatest impact."[1]

However, this boom in the utilization of the family therapy modality has not been without its drawbacks. It has given rise to the development of narrow sectarian entrenchments, esoteric language, dogmatic formularies, and a proselytizing stance. Today, there is not one family therapy but several, arising out of different theoretical formulations or, as I prefer to think, on different points of entry into the family system.

For those wishing to learn about family therapy, this problem is compounded by a rapidly changing focus in the family therapy literature from theoretical conceptualizations to empirical and methodological issues. This shift of focus is an important development. Nevertheless, for those not familiar with the theoretical conceptualizations of the authors or with the several theoretical frames of reference in the field, this could, indeed, cause bewilderment. This is no small problem, as our therapeutic perception and behavior are influenced by our theoretical orientation. A therapist's method of intervening can be understood only when seen in relation to his theory.

It is this lack of theoretical reference in the family therapy literature today that has prompted me to attempt to delineate the major theoretical positions in the field and to identify the practice techniques associated with them. To accomplish this, I shall attempt to identify those points on which there is agreement and those points regarding which there is divergence in opinion. It is my own thinking that these theoretical positions are not as diverse or as mutually exclusive as some of their proponents insist. I propose, in fact, that if the tenets of each family therapy sect were translated into a common language, a continuum of mutually supportive theories would ensue.

One explanation for the lack of a single theoretical structure can be attributed to the multiple origins of family therapy. On the East Coast, it grew out of the psychoanalytic movement while on the West Coast, it grew out of research into the nature and causation of schizophrenia. Later, work with the lower socioeconomic group gave rise to an even newer derivation.

The consequence of this lack of unitary background has been the development of the three principal theoretical schools of family therapy: a) the Psychodynamic, (b) Communications, and (c) the Structural.

Erickson and Hogan wrote that "the only overriding factor integrating the various theoretical approaches has been the continuing focus on the family as a functioning unit."[2] In an effort to formulate a working definition of family therapy which would be acceptable to all family therapists, David Olson suggested that "any intervention focussing on the family system rather than the persons in it, merits the name of family therapy."[3]

This concept of the family as a unit, a dynamic system and not just a group of individuals, is the central unifying concept in family therapy today. The family, then, is like a molecule which has an identity of its own which differs from the atoms from which it is built. Two hydrogen atoms and one oxygen atom, with the aid of a catalyst, interact in such a way that a molecule of water, a new system, results. An important characteristic of the molecule is its stability, resulting from the continuous interaction of the atoms. In the family, this stability, or balance, is called homeostasis: the dynamic, coordinated interaction of the members to maintain the family's internal stability.

When this homeostasis, the coordinated interaction of the members, is of such a configuration that it provides for the age-appropriate needs of each member, it can be called a functional family. And when the configuration of the homeostasis does not sustain all of its members in this way, the family is considered dysfunctional. Homeostasis is not equivalent to being functional or "well," but a family out of homeostasis *is* in a state of "crisis."

Any member of the family manifesting difficulty, for example, schizophrenia, behavior problems in school, anorexia nervosa, is viewed not as a patient in need of treatment but as a symptom-bearer of a dysfunctional family. Consequently, the family system as a whole and not the symptomatic member is the target for change in family therapy. This focus on the family interactional system as the target for change, instead of on an individual member, is family therapy's most important contribution to the field of mental health. It is, also, at this point that the three schools of family therapy seem to part company.

Having agreed that the family interactional system should be changed, family therapists had to determine how that system functioned in order to know how to change it and to what to change it. Separate and uncoordinated attempts to determine the nature of family interaction turned men of science into sectarian defenders of the true faith. A Tower of Babel effect resulted in the development of different languages and the breakdown of communication.

THE PSYCHODYNAMIC SCHOOL

Nathan Ackerman, Norman Paul, Ivan Boszormenyi-Nagy, and others identified with the psychodynamic school, viewed family therapy as the most recent development in psychoanalytic personality theory, which is to be distinguished from psychoanalysis as a specific treatment technique. They viewed psychoanalysis as a psychological theory initiated by Freud and further developed by others such as Klein, Fairbairn, and Sullivan. Klein and Fairbairn focused their attention on the preoedipal period of the individual's intrapsychic development in relation to the perceived experience with the needed objects in the external world, for example, breast, mother. These perceived experiences became introjected, and through the process of projection, affected subsequent perceptions of the external world, accompanied by a reexperience of the original feelings, which affected the individual's behavior in relation to others. Sullivan focused his attention on the interface of individual psyches as it affected interpersonal relationships, which earned his contribution the label of "interpersonal theory." Although these two theoretical expansions lacked developmental contiguity, they provided a theoretical continuity which enabled psychoanalytic psychology to encompass the concept of the family as a system of psychic interaction.

NATHAN ACKERMAN

Although Ackerman experienced conflict over the concept of the family as a system, he, in fact, delineates a system when he states ". . . the behavior of father, mother, or child cannot be evaluated in a social vacuum or in the exclusive context of parent-child interaction but must, rather, be regarded as a functional expression of the total interpersonal experience that characterizes the life of the family."[4]

His personal synthesis of personality theory made use of Freudian dynamics for understanding the internal processes together with what appears to be a Sullivanian emphasis on the adaptational view of personality, man in society. In 1966, he wrote:

> One is concerned here with the "live past," not the "dead past," that part of the past which is a determining force in the "here and now" experience. Of special importance is the therapist's constant striving to watch inner and outer experience, intrapersonal and interpersonal conflict, unconscious and conscious material, fantasy and reality.[5]

To explain the interactional dynamics of the family, Ackerman utilized the concept of roles in the family which he saw as always being complementary or reciprocal. In other words, there is a need-fulfillment relationship between the members of the family. If there is a failure of complementarity or reciprocity of roles, the family will not function smoothly, which gives rise to conflict and pathology.

The "failure of complementarity" is the corollary of "misunderstandings, confusions, and distortions" which are the product of "the old deviant patterns of alignment."[6]

Family dysfunction, then, is seen by Ackerman as a failure in the reciprocal need-fulfillment relationships in the family. His therapeutic goal is to change the role relationships within the family to effect a more satisfactory homeostasis. To accomplish this end, he attempts to disrupt the pathogenic homeostasis, which is, in effect, "crisis-inducing therapy," a concept now popular with Minuchin. With the dysfunctional homeostasis disrupted, a new pattern can replace it.

Ackerman himself described this whole process with great clarity:

> The open, forthright approach of the therapist, his use of confrontation, and the device called "tickling the defenses," often startles the family members into a greater awareness; it forces them to face up to the issues. It penetrates resistances and cuts through habitual avoidance, denials, and barriers to sharing the struggle with conflict. Temporarily, the sense of personal exposure and the titter of anxiety is heightened, but the noxious effects are at the same time counterbalanced by an offering of greater acceptance, understanding and support. The use of these uncovering methods shakes up established alignments and splits in the family group. In so doing, it disorganizes the preexisting pathogenic equilibrium of relationships, while making way for new kinds of coping and readaptation of family role reciprocity at an improved and healthier level.[7]

In the process of achieving this end, Ackerman utilized communication theory, emphasizing that all behavior was communication, even the seating arrangement chosen by the family in the therapy room.

NORMAN PAUL

While Norman Paul declares his theoretical ties to Freud and Sullivan, it is the object-relations dimension of his theory which strikes me as the most prominent. Paul examines the interacting family system by focusing on the architects of the system, the husband and wife. He considers that the mate selection itself is affected by the needs of the individual man and woman in relation to their own experiences with their families of origin. Maladaptive responses to a perceived object and part-object loss in the past results in a symbiotic fixity in role relationships, causing inappropriate reaction to each other. Such perceived losses and associated sense of deprivation lead to a residue of sorrow, anger, grief, guilt, bitterness, despair, and regret. "These affects," writes Paul, "timeless as experienced internally, appear to dictate a restitutive response characterized by the emergence of a perceptual set leading to mate selection."[8] It is as if each seeks in the other what is perceived to have been lost. The outcome of this mating is an oscillating marital homeostasis associated with a denial of, or a warding off of, real or imagined losses, disappointments, or major changes, and the concomitant defensive maneuvers. The rupture or distancing which results in the marital diad affects the relationship which each parent has with each child and the relationship which the children have with each other. It is this homeostatic configuration which Paul considers to be the family pathology which gives rise to symptomatic individuals who will in turn establish similar marriages.

Because incomplete mourning for the lost love-object is the cause of the family dysfunction, Paul considers that completing the mourning process would free the individuals to meet each other's realistic needs and establish a new and more fulfilling homeostasis. This technique of inducing a belated mourning reaction is referred to as "operational mourning."

"Operational mourning" calls for repeated inquiry about remembered losses and accompanying affect in an effort to elicit the exposure of intense feelings in the individual involved. Having accomplished this, the therapist focuses on the feelings which this aroused in the other partner. Utilizing his own ability to empathize with the pained member, he attempts to help the spouse "resonate empathetically with the belated mourner."[9] This experience of the sense of loss, accompanied by the empathetic feelings of the mate, has, in Paul's experiments, led to the recall of almost forgotten experiences of loss.

Family therapy as conducted by Paul calls for the induction of "operational mourning" in both partners. Although Paul's focus is on the marital diad, his goal is to effect change in the whole family interactional system. Change in the parental interaction effects change in the entire interactional configuration.

IVAN BOSZORMENYI-NAGY

Ivan Boszormenyi-Nagy sees the family interactional system as combinations of diadic relationships. These relationships are based on the individual's private fictions about the meaning of the relationship with that particular other in terms of need-fulfillment. Needs come in two varieties: (a) "need for an object of one's drives, and (b) needs for an object of one's specific need configuration as a basis of self-delineation."[10]

The first need is growth-related and is realistic and age-appropriate—what I prefer to call "growth needs." When a man and woman need each other for companionship, intimacy, and sex, or when parents need the satisfaction of seeing their children grow into self-sustaining adult persons, while the child needs their support and encouragement to attain that state, there are mutual relationships based on the need for an object of one's drives.

The second need is what he calls "ontic" dependence on a certain other. It is what I call "deficit needs," implying that these are needs left over from an earlier period of development. Boszormenyi-Nagy explains that this need means "that my full self-meaning depends on a fitting other."[11]

The desired homeostasis of diadic relationships consists of a "dialogue of needs which guarantees that the relationship will not turn into a one-sided exploitation."[12] He sees a struggle for mastery among the family members in their individual efforts to manipulate each other to act in accordance with their private relational needs and expectations. (You will note the strong similarity between this concept and the ideas of Jay Haley.) This struggle for dominance or control of the relationship affects the nature of the husband-wife dyad and ultimately the parent-children diads. The ambivalent attitudes which this type of relationship can produce may give rise to a communicational system of contradictory messages which Bateson, Jackson, and Haley call the "double bind."

Boszormenyi-Nagy sees relationships based on "ontic needs" leading to "unconsciously collusive motivational systems" which may result in what Murray Bowen describes as an "undifferentiated family ego mass."

As his stated therapeutic goal he tries to effect "self-confirmation" in the individual family members to permit the development of diadic relationships based on reciprocal transactions of mutual "possession," and to move away from "amorphous fusion."

THE COMMUNICATIONS SCHOOL

The Communication theorists were all associated with the Mental Research Center in Palo Alto, California, where they discovered that schizophrenia was a product of family homeostasis or rather, an integral part of the homeostatic balance of the schizophrenic's family. They determined, also, that the interactional equilibrium was the product of the family communicational pattern.

Communication should not be taken here to mean only verbal communication but also, non-verbal communication. Behavior itself is considered communication. As Don Jackson said, "one cannot not communicate."[13] Everything that happens in a family is communication and is significant.

Although united by this theoretical concept, there is a wide divergence in the various applications of the theory. Because of the immediate association of their names with communication theory, I have selected Don Jackson, Jay Haley, and Virginia Satir to represent this school.

DON JACKSON

Don Jackson contributed more to the theoretical conceptualization of the family as a dynamic homeostatic system than any other family therapist. Both the terms "system" and "homeostasis" were first applied to the family by him. Also, it was out of the research program which he headed that many other widely accepted concepts in family therapy developed such as that of "double bind communication," and "metacommunication."

When we return to our basic question of how the family system functions, we come to a significant apparent divergence between the psychodynamic theorists and Jackson. While Jackson would not deny the existence of the intrapsychic, he would declare that it had no relevance to family therapy. "Why" members of the family functioned or communicated in a particular way was of no concern to him but only "how" they functioned or communicated. He used the "black box concept" to explain his position. To recast his explanation of this concept in modern terms, he was not interested in knowing about the complex inner workings of a computer but only in the input-output of the mechanism.

To Jackson, "the family is an interacting communications network in which every member from the day-old baby to the seventy-year-old grandfather influences the nature of the entire system and in turn is influenced by it."[14]

In spite of Jackson's rejection of the "why" of family interaction, when he talks about the three factors which are operative in the initial stage of the development of the family system, he seems to be considering the "why" of interaction. The first factor is the individual's goals for the marriage, which Jackson states are both conscious and unconscious—for example, status and approval. This coming together of two sets of goals will develop into a joint system of goals. The second factor is the choice of mate, which will itself limit the goals of the family by means of education, wealth, age, and family contacts. The third factor is the initial type of family structure resulting from each spouse's attempting to determine and control the nature of the relationship. (This concept is very similar to the one proposed by Boszormenyi-Nagy.) Each spouse wants to have his or her goals (needs) fulfilled without having to reciprocate or take the needs of the other into account. But eventually, a family homeostasis is achieved through a process of "quid pro quo" bargaining. Later, when a child enters the family, the homeostasis will again be disrupted and a new one negotiated. The "quid pro quo" pattern of establishing and maintaining homeostasis "becomes an unwritten (usually not consciously recognized) set of ground rules."[15] Violation of the rules means disruption of the homeostasis, which means trouble, because it leads to a dysfunctional homeostasis. For the system to survive, there is need for mutual responsibility, reward, security, and dignity.[16]

In his interventions to right the family homeostasis, Jackson intervenes in order to disrupt the dysfunctional homeostasis. The techniques which he applies are those derived from communication theory such as: (a) *Relabeling*—taking the motivation that has been labeled in a negative way and labeling it in a positive way . . .,"[17] (b) *Prescribing the Symptom*—telling the person to act as he or she has been acting. Haley calls this the "paradoxical injunction." Insight is an important aspect of Jackson's approach. What one thinks, influences one's behavior. Consequently, when one understands what is going wrong in the interactional system, he can choose to change it.

JAY HALEY

Haley sees the family as a homeostatic, cybernetic communicational system in which the goal of each member is to define or control the relationship. This power struggle is the essence of all relationships, for Haley sees the individual person involved in a constant effort to establish his "influence and control over his social world" and to make that "world more predictable."[18]

Relationships are established and maintained through cybernetic communication or a circular, as opposed to linear, communication system. Haley writes, "When one person communicates a message to another, he is maneuvering to define the relationship."[19] This power struggle in the family system is the central concept of Haley's approach to family therapy. It is also his answer to the question of how the family interactional system functions. The family is a homeostatic balance of the individual member's constant attempt to be in control through communication.

Communication, of course, is not just verbal but also nonverbal. All behavior is communication. But there are levels of communication which modify each other. Thus, for example, it is not just what is said that is important but rather, the second level of communication which tells how to interpret the first level of communication. This is the notion of "metacommunication," which means the communication about the communication. A mother, for example, might tell her son that he must not steal and yet lets him know that she had put in an order for a "hot" bicycle for him for Christmas. In effect, her metacommunication said, "Cancel the message about not stealing."

Haley sees the "identified patient" as scapegoat of the family power struggle. Pathology in the family means pathology of the "communication system," alias power struggle. He claims that pathology is interpersonal rather than intrapsychic. "Psychopathology," he writes, "is a product of a power struggle between persons rather than between internal forces. This shift from conflict within to conflict without requires a major rethinking of psychiatric theory."[20] He outlines this shift of thinking with a hypothetical example:

> Let us say that an adolescent commits some delinquent act, such as stealing a car. . . . When we try to explain his motive for the act, our explanations will differ with our unit of observation.

> If our unit is the boy, we must explain that he stole the car because of something about him and his nature. . . . He is immoral . . . he has a weak conscience . . . he is expressing feelings of adolescent rebellion against the establishment, or that he lacks impulse control . . .

> If we think in terms of a dyad, we would include at least two people in our description. We might say that the act was done in relationship to a peer, or we could say that his mother or his father were not firm enough in giving him proper discipline . . . or his father encouraged this kind of behavior because he got vicarious satisfaction out of the boy's misbehavior.

> Should the investigator make his description in terms of three people, he will describe the act as part of a triangular interchange. For example . . . when a marital couple is about to break up and seek a divorce, their child will get into difficulty in some way. The parents pull back together to deal with the problem child and the marriage stabilizes."[21]

Although Haley sees this concept as a radical shift, Ackerman had already formulated this concept under the rubric of "family healer" when describing a child's pathology as a means of keeping the parents together.

When Haley discusses his techniques for changing the family, once again, we are presented with the technique of disrupting the existing homeostasis in order to enable a less pathogenic one to be constituted. His approach to accomplishing this task is to offer the family ". . . an educational factor to help them behave differently and therapeutic paradoxes to force them to do so."

Paradoxical communication is an intrinsic factor in Haley's approach to family therapy. His tactics include: (a) ambiguous directives to the family, (b) emphasis on the positive—relabeling as with Jackson, (c) encouraging the usual behavior—paradoxical injunction.

The therapist creates a situation in which: (1) there is a benevolent framework in which change is to take place, (2) unchanged behavior is permitted, (3) an ordeal will continue as long as the behavior remains unchanged.[22]

VIRGINIA SATIR

Virginia Satir is well known for her major contribution to the field of family therapy: in her book, *Conjoint Family Therapy*, she identifies the four conceptual building blocks of her theoretical orientation: (1) self-esteem, (2) communication, (3) system, and (4) rules.

Self-esteem relates to the emotional maturation level of the individual. A mature person is self-delineated and self-determined. In Bowen's terms, he is not enmeshed in the "undifferentiated family ego mass." A mature person makes choices based on an accurate perception of himself and others. Satir equates self-esteem to self-image and self-worth and accounts for its presence or absence in terms of the individual's experiences within his family of origin. On this point she states, "If parents consistently show that they consider their child as a masterful, sexual person, and if they also demonstrate a gratifying, functional male-female relationship, the child acquires self-esteem and becomes increasingly independent of his parents."[23]

Conversely, the child who did not experience this affirmation of his self-worth will experience a sense of low self-esteem. (This position places Satir in very close proximity to the object-relations theorists.)

When choosing a mate, the individual who has a sense of high self-esteem will select a person on a similar level of maturity in order to enhance his feeling of self-worth in a relationship of complementarity. On the other hand, the person of low self-esteem will search out someone who will supply him with what he is missing. In object-relations language, he is seeking the lost object. Through a complex process of self-deception and dysfunctional communication, he succeeds in joining someone akin to himself in feelings of poor self-worth. The result is a sense of dissatisfaction.

With the birth of a child, a triangulation process is initiated with each parent seeking from the child what he or she cannot get from each other. In the words of Satir, "Both mates look to the child to satisfy their unmet needs in the marital relationship." In this way, the diadic system which was in danger of splitting apart has been replaced by a triadic one in which the child serves the purpose of keeping the family together. A new homeostasis is established around the child and is maintained through the family communication system. The product of this is a set of family rules mostly outside of conscious awareness which governs the family's business of interacting. "In a family a rule may be that only good things may be said and only good feelings expressed."[24]

Change in the interactional pattern of the family is accomplished by uncovering the covert family rules—the rules about self and self-manifestation, about self and the expectation of others, about self and the outside world. Through this process of exposing the family rules, Satir holds that the family is thereby free to change the rules to allow for greater fulfillment and growth.

Her approach to uncovering the family rules is to focus on the communicational patterns of the family, which as with Jackson and Haley, includes all behavior in the family.

THE STRUCTURAL SCHOOL

SALVADOR MINUCHIN

Salvador Minuchin is the architect of what has become known as Structural Family Therapy. He perceives the family as "a natural social system which has evolved ways of organizing and transacting that are economical and effective for that particular group."[25] In this statement, we see the dual concepts of "family system" and "family homeostasis."

The family seeks help when the system's coping and adaptive mechanisms are obstructed by stress overloads on the system, resulting in some symptomatic behavior in one of their members.

The source of the stress may be internal or external, arising from problems related to the transitional stage of the family's development, the transition of a member to adolescence, the arrival of a new family member, the departure of a member, a child's problems in school, the father's loss of a job, etc. It could also develop from poverty, discrimination, or from separation from a natural support system.

Minuchin rejects the psychodynamic approach of looking at present transactions as projections of the past, with therapeutic change seen in terms of cutting loose from the past. He takes an existential position and states that the past exists in the present organization and functioning and is currently "available to change-producing interventions."[26]

The main focus of structural family therapy, as the name implies, is the family structure. Family sets are the structural units of ultimate importance. Minuchin defines "sets" as "patterned sequences of interaction among family members" and family pathology as "the development of dysfunctional sets."[27] Dysfunctional sets are nonproblem-resolving reactions to stress which are repeated without modification. Adaptation of the family is blocked by such sets.

Dysfunctional sets can involve diads, triads, or the entire family, and even extra-familial systems. Minuchin gives the hypothetical example of a child who is emerging into adolescence while simultaneously increasing his status in the extra-familial world. Problems around control and autonomy therefore develop within the family. The relationship between the adolescent and his mother resists the changes necessary for adaptation. Mother attacks adolescent; father defends adolescent; the other children enter the conflict. This dysfunctional set will be repeated in every new stressful situation.

To change the family system, the therapist must first determine the structure of the family in terms of dysfunctional sets and areas of strength. Based on this assessment, he determines his priorities for intervention, sets his goals, and considers his therapeutic options and strategies.

Based on configurations of dysfunctional sets, several types of systems have been identified. *Enmeshed families* are composed of members who are too involved in each other's lives. The "perverse triangle" is one set in such a family, involving a crossgenerational alliance which excludes another member of either generation. In intervening in such a family, the objective would be to create an emotional barrier between the generations. The techniques utilized to accomplish this end would be: (a) "weaken the existing cross-generational alliance; (b) develop a stronger parental coalition; (c) assist both parents and children to extend and strengthen relationships with peers at their own generational level."[28]

Disengaged families are families in which the members have minimal effective impact on each other. The goal of therapy with such a family is to increase the influence which family members have on each other. Techniques to be used in this case would include: (a) facilitating accurate communication with meaningful feedback; (b) clarify family rules and procedures for enforcement; (c) define clear role relationships among family members.

The overall interventive approach of structural family therapy is not to effect insight, or improve communication, or even bring about emotional discharge but rather, to change family structures in terms of changing dysfunctional sets into functional ones. The approach could best be described as "engineered change." Most frequently, the family will not even know what has really happened to them or even what was wrong in the first place. Manipulation of the system is probably the most apt way of describing structural family therapy—planned manipulation.

CONCLUSION

If for a moment we were to forget the various sectarian splits in family therapy and attempt to develop a theory based on what we have been presented by each school, could we not decide on something approximating the following theoretical statement?

Due to experiences of emotional deprivation in the early stages of development, reinforced through the repetition of dysfunctional sets during subsequent stages of development, a person might reach adulthood with a sense of low self-esteem and a determination to have others fulfill his deficit needs.

Such a person would select a mate who showed promise of meeting the unmet needs but would most likely choose someone like himself with low self-esteem. This relationship would result in a homeostatic balance, with each member utilizing power maneuvers in communicating to force the other to fulfill the deficit needs. With the arrival of a child, triangulation would ensue, with each parent competing for the love of the child. This would cause cross-generational enmeshment with the probable outcome of the child being absorbed in the undifferentiated family ego mass.

To intervene in such a family, several points of entry could be identified, each calling for different therapeutic techniques.

One might intervene with each member of the marital pair to reach and release the residues of affect connected with the original sense of loss, and effect a therapeutic mourning enabling the person to separate from the lost object, thus facilitating natural growth development, resulting in interactional change among the family members.

Or intervention could be at the system level, which might involve various techniques aimed at disrupting the homeostasis.

Intervention might also focus on the communicational patterns to uncover the family rules and thereby, change them. It might even focus on the dysfunctional sets with the goal of engineering more functional sets.

This, of course, is a very simplistic attempt at a unified theory of family therapy. Nevertheless, it does suggest that such a unification is possible if the sectarian stance were replaced by an honest search for a theoretical "rapprochement."

FOOTNOTES

1. Alan S. Gurman, Ph.D., "Marital Therapy: Emerging Trends in Research and Practice," *Family Process* (March 1973), Vol. 12, No. 1, p. 45.
2. Gerald Erickson, Terrence Hogan, *Family Therapy: An Introduction to Theory and Technique* (Berkley, 1972), p. 49.
3. David Olson, quoted by Vincent D. Foley, M.D., *An Introduction to Family Therapy* (New York, 1974), p. 3.
4. Nathan Ackerman, *The Psychodynamics of Family Life* (New York, 1958), p. 22.
5. *Ibid.*, p. 42.
6. Nathan Ackerman, *Treating the Troubled Family* (New York, 1966), p. 39.
7. Nathan Ackerman, "Family Psychotherapy Today: Some Areas of Controversy," *Comprehensive Psychiatry* (October, 1966). Vol. 7, No. 5, p. 381.
8. Norman Paul, M.D., "The Role of Mourning and Empathy in Conjoint Marital Therapy," *Family Therapy and Disturbed Families*, Gerald H. Zuk and Ivan Boszormenyi-Nagy (eds.) (Palo Alto, California, 1969), p. 188.
9. *Ibid.*, p. 189.
10. Ivan Boszormenyi-Nagy, "Relational Modes of Meaning," *Family Therapy and Disturbed Families* (Palo Alto, California,) p. 60.
11. *Ibid.*
12. *Ibid.*
13. P. Watzlawick, J. Beavin, D. Jackson, *Pragmatics of Human Communication* (New York, 1967), p. 48.
14. Lederer, D. Jackson, *The Mirages of Marriage* (New York, 1968), p. 14.
15. *Ibid.*, p. 179.
16. *Ibid.*, p. 11.
17. Jackson, D. "The Eternal Triangle," in *Techniques of Family Therapy*, J. Haley & L. Hoffman, (eds.) (New York, 1967), p. 200.
18. J. Haley, *The Power Tactics of Jesus Christ* (New York, 1969), p. 36.
19. J. Haley, "An Interactional Description of Schizophrenia," *Psychiatry* (1959), Vol. 22, p. 323.
20. J. Haley, *Strategies of Psychotherapy* (New York, 1963,) p. 156.
21. J. Haley, "Family Therapy: A Radical Change," in *Changing Families*, Jay Haley (ed.) (New York, 1971), pp. 277-278.
22. J. Haley, *Strategies of Psychotherapy*, p. 181.
23. V. Satir, *Conjoint Family Therapy* (Palo Alto, California, 1967), p. 53.
24. Vincent Foley, Ph.D., *An Introduction to Family Therapy* (New York, 1974), p. 100.

25. Salvador Minuchin, *Structural Family Therapy.* Unpublished manuscript, p. 1.

26. *Ibid.,* p. 2.

27. *Ibid.,* p. 4.

28. Howard Camp, M.S.W., "Structural Family Therapy: An Outsider's Perspective," *Family Process* (1973), p. 270.

TOWARD A NEW FORMULATION OF OBJECT RELATION-SYSTEMS THEORY FROM ANALYSIS AND FAMILY ECOLOGY THEORIES

Ed Leonhard

INTRODUCTION

For some time, I have had an interest in two areas of personality theory and therapy—the intrapsychic and extrapsychic orientations. In this paper, I am proposing a possible new theory because each of these approaches appears to me to contain certain lacunae in themselves. Both the intra- and extrapsychic therapies have been warring needlessly in childish competition with each other during a great deal of their history. Who, for example, hasn't seen a family therapist get up on stage and ridicule analysis and vice versa? However, I have always felt quite comfortable in practicing and teaching both psychoanalysis and family therapy.

However, my interest in both approaches regarding their possible theoretical interactional contributions to one another never became more accentuated than when two things happened to me several years ago. First, I became a faculty member in a medical residency psychiatric training program in which I have been teaching and supervising residents in both modalities simultaneously. And secondly, I have begun to supervise them in crisis intervention. The former happening helped focus my interest on both approaches; the latter forced me to emphasize and concentrate more on the extreme extrapsychic traditions in family therapy's ecological systems theory in attempting to adopt family therapy systems theory into a more effective approach to crisis

42

work. While doing this, I realized certain inadequacies and blind spots in using merely a systems-oriented theory and therapy in solving people's crises and the need to include analytic insights in helping them to cope with their critical problems.

That I started becoming more intrigued with the intersections between these two approaches is not unusual for me. Commonalities among various systems of thought have always interested me far more than their differences. Little wonder, then, that my favorite thinkers have for a while been Teilhard de Chardin and R. Buckminster Fuller. As a result of these interests, I spent a week many years ago living and dialoguing with Dr. Fuller in a small house in Connecticut. (Teilhard couldn't accommodate me since he's been busy, taken up with the experience of the Omega Point for many years now.) At that time, I was inducted into the former's evolutionary world view. I began to look at reality through a sort of reversed pair of binoculars. Through them, I was given a precious world view not only of the planet's continuing evolutionary history but also, of the other more day-to-day institutions that have interfaced with my life and work since then. One of the more practical areas that this colloquium prepared me for was my pursuit in obtaining this theoretical interaction, namely, the intrapsychic and the extrapsychic, the results of which led to this paper.

Before proceeding, however, a warning! It is my style not to spend time researching and then footnoting what I write. I enjoy, rather, concentrating all of my efforts on developing my own personal intuitive reactions to things as they come to me rather than to use up time searching out whether or not others have discussed similar formulations. (Thus, it was only a few weeks before the presentation of this paper that I discovered purely by accident that the first international meeting on psychoanalysis and family therapy would be addressing my topic in Philadelphia on the very day I would be discussing my own thoughts on the possible results of the interrelatedness of these two therapies.) The considerations in this presentation are, therefore, abstract, often arising from esoteric concepts that none the less interest me.

With this said, let me first outline the two major thoughts that seemed to lead me to the proposal of this new theoretical posture. Then, I will present the proposed theory that is the central message of this paper.

THEORETICAL PREDECESSORS AND BRIDGES TO THIS THEORY

FAMILY ECOLOGY THEORY

I call the type of crisis intervention that I teach to our trainees *Family Ecology Therapy*. *Ecology*—to describe the approach that is employed in order to plan the correct interventions needed to help the clients deal with the crisis, and *family*—in order to define the therapeutic tool and modality used to put into effect the planned interventions within the parameters of the actual contacts with the clients in therapy sessions. Now, ecology is obviously not used in the sense of cleaning up the environment but rather, in the sense of viewing the beginnings and ends of the crisis problem and all of the converging forces that come together to effect a condition of disorganization in a system that shows up as a crisis in one part or member of that system. In commenting about the ecological approach, some authors are quick to point out that it incorporates the Eastern nonlinear type of causality and not the linear cause-and-effect scientific thinking that has permeated so much of the Western therapy and personality model. I tend to take a bit of exception to this definition of ecology because I think it is only partly true. There is no doubt that the ecological orientation does include the viewing of the therapeutic problem and the search for its solutions in a holistic approach but it also is ecological enough I would hope, to include and allow for linear, more traditional psychodynamic causes as well as converging, nonlinear ones. If it doesn't, it wouldn't be a truly ecological approach because some crises in a system can rightfully be traced to both linear and nonlinear models.

Let me explain this and the ecological orientation with a brief therapy example. A local grammar school calls up our crisis team to report that they have an emergency. A young boy in school has just violently attacked another and they need our help. The crisis team responds and gathers the following ecological perspective before planning their interventions. It has been two months since the youngster began acting out in this violent way. At that time, the Mother's lover had been invited to come live with her and this, her only son. Simultaneously, the Matriarch of the Mother's family network had been invited by her to come in everyday to babysit for the boy. This Grandmother had often maintained that her daughter did not raise children properly, and now, she was determined to prove her point through understanding and permissiveness contrary to the Mother's methods. The boyfriend had just come out of the army and believed in heavy discipline as the solution. In addition, he had for some time been having an argument with the principal in the school because he saw him as being too permissive and not giving a high quality of education to ghetto children. Needless to say, the Mother found herself in the middle of these converging forces and unsure where she stood as an "I" person. There were other inputs, for example, with the boy's teacher, etc., but these suffice.

Now, as a team with ecological "goggles" on, it is important to note that no one else in that entire case had the complete view of the forces which were interacting in a nonlinear, mutual, amplifying, closed system to generate multiple tensions and problems. More importantly, therefore, no one else in the system, except for the ecologically-tuned crisis team, could effectively deal with these converging forces. The team then used the family part of family ecology therapy to implement the ecological phase and employed the techniques of family network therapy to effect the planned changes.

Briefly, the team held a network session with the principal, the Mother, the surrogate Father-boyfriend and worked out a better working alliance with the surrogate and principal. They promised to help Mother, surrogate-Father, and boy with the family-based problems (thus alleviating the fears of the school people) and did so by instructing the new Father to share his own boyhood acting out problems with his new son. As a result of this ensuing closeness of Father and Son, the Father had no need merely to depend on punitive discipline because he saw other solutions as quite viable, and the boy stopped acting out. A family network session worked through the possible sabotaging effects (systemically unconscious, of course) of the Matriarch.

In the ecological view, I feel that this example demonstrates not only systems causality but also, more traditional linear causality. To be ecological and deny the psychodynamic Western cause-and-effect model is, in my opinion, as I've already said, to return to as narrowminded a parochial (and what is worse, non-ecological) view as one is trying to correct. Consequently, in addition to their systems intervention, the crisis team uncovered psychodynamic unresolved Oedipal problems in the boy and recommended treatment for that as part of the overall crisis work. Time unfortunately does not permit any further description of the extrapsychic, ecological theoretical stance at this time and in this paper. I would like to turn now to a short description of the other theoretical posture leading to the new proposed theory of Object Relation-Systems Theory.

ANALYTIC OBJECT RELATION THEORY

There is today a burgeoning branch of analytic intrapsychic thinking that offers in its essential theoretical givens a natural and ideal bridge to family-ecology therapy, thus preparing the way, in my opinion, for the new theory this paper presents. It is the object relations theory of Fairbairn, Winicott, and Guntrip. As it has generated increasing interest here in the States for a while now, I am confident that I need not go into any details about it. The very name cries out to be connected to the theory of ecology systems. For object relations analytic theory focuses in on the various relational realities within the unconscious of the person as well as the people-objects that go to make up the phenomenological private universe of the person that is outside the parameters of the unconscious. It chooses not to adopt the foci of the earlier Freud such as the instinctual erogenous zones, or the mechanistic theory, or geographical concepts of ego, id, and superego that would make any connection to systems thinking very tenuous and unproductive at most.

A PROPOSAL FOR AN OBJECT
RELATION-SYSTEMS THEORY

At one time or another, theoreticians seem compelled to address themselves to the question of where do emotional problems dwell. In the case of the two theories just briefly outlined, the choices are clear. The given posture of the theory almost, as it were, predetermines where the particular school of therapy and of personality will locate the answer. In the case of analysis, emotional problems are seen as existing in both the unconscious and conscious of the person; in the case of family therapy, in the nuclear, extended (both as to relationships and time parameters), and network family systems.

In my opinion, the question opens up useless polemics. I say "useless" because I think the question is a nonquestion. For in dealing with emotional conflicts, we are dealing with them as they exist in various hierarchical systems and subsystems. Thus, emotional problems exist in all of the various systems in which the humanoid is found. A family can be disorganized and manifest an emotional problem on the family level, and a person can likewise become disorganized as a person-system and reveal conflicts. The particular problem on a higher hierarchical level such as a family can reverberate in a mutual causal way within the parts or entities of that higher system, namely, the people-objects that comprise that family. Similarly, the parts that go to make up the subsystem, such as the individual family members, can through mutual causality, effect and bring about an emotional problem in the family's higher system in what I would call system-projection. Or for that matter, the person could, for example, be considered a system of which the unconscious is a particular subsystem. One then could look for emotional difficulties in the conscious person and any disintegration that may be taking place within the organization of the ego, or one could look at the subsystem of the unconscious and examine the conflicts that are transpiring there. Obviously, in this case too, the boundaries of the systems and therefore, the mutual interactions of the problems of one system onto another are very fluid and mutually interacting.

Consequently, it is a waste of time for the family theoretician to lay claim to emotional problems as residing only within the family structure or for the analyst theoretician to say they reside only within the individual person's conscious or unconscious system. Similarly, in the area of therapeutic intervention, because of the general system principle of equifinality, it is just as ridiculous for one modality to say that the proper way to intervene in order to bring about healing is within the particular system that his or her theory concentrates on. Let me explain.

In an open system, which, by the way, is what a person or a family normally is, the same final characteristic state or goal, if you will, may be arrived at from different initial states and in different ways. This is so because in open systems, things are caused not in linear ways but in mutually interacting ways, and the same final goal may be reached in different interacting causal ways. Two modalities approaching the same therapeutic healing-goal but from two different system approaches may achieve the same goal. Thus, a family therapist can relieve the depression of a family, and therefore, of the persons going to make up that system, and an individual within that larger family system. (Naturally, it must not be forgotten that the goals are often different or on a different level, and in these cases, equifinality wouldn't apply.)

The principle of equifinality, I might add, stirs up even more absurd controversies among various schools within the same theory. Thus, the structural-family therapist may solve a family problem that a systems-family therapist also solves but each from a different approach. Or two family-system therapists may solve the same problem though each may enter the family system at a different point. Both introduce system changes into the same system, cause mutually interacting systems to interact, and both achieve the same final goals.

As seen from a general systems viewpoint, there then seems to be ample theoretical reasons to say that one can propose a theory that can take into account both the person and the family unit as mutually interacting system-subsystems while allowing as a tenet of this theory that different therapeutic interventions on different levels of systems can have their legitimate and mutually valid, if you will, approaches. I would suggest, then, my first thoughts on where such a theory might lead. I choose to call it *Object Relation-Systems Theory.*

THE PROPOSED THEORY OF OBJECT RELATION-SYSTEMS

The word "object" is used because both object relation analytic theory and family theory concentrate on the objects of human beings as the primary foci of human development and therapeutic treatment. Both approaches also share a common interest not so much in these objects as in the "relationships" that exist within the entities of these object-systems. Finally, the word "system" is used because both theories approach emotional problems and their treatment on two significant levels of systems: namely, the system of the family and the subsystem of each of the persons that go to make up such network systems. Moreover, both regard their areas of interest in the family and the person as separate systems, the disorganization of which is essentially an emotional upset.

One caution: this theory is not simply a synthesis of combining of the two approaches just discussed under one conceptual umbrella. In either theory, the ideas generated are essentially different in the way that the whole is not always (often to some, unexpectedly) equal to the sum of its parts.

In this paper, then, I would like to share some of my beginning thoughts regarding Object Relation-Systems Theory but only as they relate primarily to the Individual-Person-System level and then, in a future paper, concentrate on how this theory would contribute to new ideas on the higher hierarchical family system level of organization.

THE PERSON-SYSTEM-LEVEL
IN AN OBJECT RELATION-SYSTEMS THEORY

A NEW PERCEPTION OF THE PSYCHIC-ECOLOGICAL ARENA OF THE PERSON

It would be very tempting to place and define the theoretical ecology of the person as a theory that comes out of an interaction between object relation and family system theories in two worlds: the intra- and the extrapsychic of the person. This not only would be a mistake, made all too often in personality theory because of the burden of a mistaken philosophical dichotomy, but it would be merely a summed combination of two foci. Moreover, such a dichotomy is a conceptualization which is more theoretically useful than it is an authentic representation of reality. In the theory here being proposed which purports to take into consideration both the internal and external realities of the personality and their interactions and interrelatedness within the person, it must be strongly proposed that a human being has only one phenomenal universe or reality in which both the intra- and extrapsychic components are experienced. In the general system orientation proposed by this *Object Relation-Systems Theory*, the important starting off point, it seems to me, in order to avoid monstrously artificial and inaccurate pictures, must be to see the extra- and intrapsychic realities interacting fluidly in a continuous tension within the one, unitary phenomenological cosmos called the person. To label this arena the "ego" or some equally imposed concept that theoretically fragments the one person into unreal artifacts would be to perpetuate an artificial and damaging concept. The person should be considered an open system of psychic units mutually interacting with one another in a fluid way.

SOME WAYS OF INTERACTING IN THE PERSON

It is in describing the ways psychic entities interact and not so much in insisting that the arena must be perceived as one phenomenological experience that Object Relation-Systems Theory would introduce major shifts in its proposals. The traditional analytic theory, whatever the particular branch, has often proposed one-to-one dyadic relationships in the psyche (in this case, often the unconscious). Object Relation Analytic Theory seems to have adopted this model from its parent Freudian orientation. Thus, the anti-libidinal ego can negatively relate to the libidinal ego and as in all cases of dyadic relationships, this particular interaction is seen according to a model of linear causality. So a punitive, self-defeating, anti-libidinal ego may be seen as being the cause of a particular effect such as increased depression from the conflict of the two.

I would like to propose that one of the givens of Object Relation-Systems Theory, as far as the person is concerned, would possibly be that more than just simple cause-and-effect is going on in the psyche of the person—not that it would seek to discredit or deny the existence of the cause-and-effect model so popular to the Western theoretician and therapy scientist. No, because it would be a theory that purports to be a general systems framework involving all reality, it would admit the latter. But it would also investigate other causal patterns within the phenomenological person. One proposed pattern for example, psychic entities in addition to relating to each other in dyads, are also part of a system in which the various parts relate in systemic ways as would be expected. Family systems theoreticians have for the length of their history been addressing the fact that families, and people, and all kinds of networks can be broken down basically into triangles. What is new here is that Object Relation-Systems Theory proposes that these triangles exist as introjects within the system of the person along with the dyads. Thus, one finds triangles not only in the outside environment of society where people form into groups but because the phenomenology of the person is a direct mirror of this social reality, the introjects within the person's phenomenology form likewise into triangles.

As a result of my discovering for myself these "goggles" of the Object Relation-Systems Theory, I began to perceive introjects relating in triangles in my analytic patients where heretofore I had perceived only dyadic relationships and only linear causality as previously discussed. Now, I began to see triangles in nonlinear systemic, mutually interacting causal systems. To confirm my findings that introjects tend to form as often into significant triangles within the person as they seem to do outside in society and families, I ran the following experiment for myself and some colleagues: I took a well-written case presentation that I was evaluating for a person's graduation from my analytic institute and reviewed its raw data in order to see if there were any introjected triangles to be found in it though only the traditional dyadic ones were alluded to in the case history. Lo and behold, wherever I looked they could easily be found. What had appeared to be a well-presented and thoroughly thought out process of treatment suddenly brought forth entirely new and rich materials leading to unseen insights into the dynamics of the case.

Another interesting concept forms once Object Relation-Systems Theory posits the existence of triangles within the phenomenology of the person. This happens as a direct result of the fact that this theory perceives them as one psychic reality in which the introjected psychic entities (which I will describe in the next section) fluidly interact with each other according to laws of systems. Let me offer just some of the myriad and rich possibilities which the properly attuned therapist might encounter in one adult client as being experienced within his Person.

One introject could be triangulated with two extrojects (an extroject being defined as an objectively real object that has been introjected and now perceived within the one phenomenological psyche of the person). Thus, an introjected anti-libidinal ego which demands passivity might be within the person in a triangle with the following two extrojects: a boss who is demanding aggressive action and a fellow worker who is trying to sabotage such aggressive business behavior because he wants to be the one to advance his career in the eyes of the boss, thus causing anxiety. Or two introjects (formerly perceived in dyadic conflict by the therapist) may be triangulated with an extroject. Or three introjects may be in a mutual deviation-amplifying triangle with each other such as two antithetical anti-libidinal egos triangulated with an active central ego (Guntrip). Or three extrojects may be triangulated with one another. (This is the typical psychic phenomena that is focused in on by the family systems and family ecologist therapist with one major difference: in the theory proposed in this paper, the Object Relation-Systems therapist perceives this triangle and its parts not as they truly exist in so-called objective reality but rather, as they are distorted to appear in the reality of the client in his own phenomenological universe within his person. The difference can often be startling and the conclusions made by even the family therapist critically significant!) Finally, there is one last general possibility of triangulation. Triangles can easily triangulate with other triangles and mutually interact with themselves within the person.

I will not go into the various laws of triangular relationships here; they have been amply and brilliantly written about by countless family-systems theoreticians. Suffice it to say that these system dynamics equally apply to the relationships of the psychic entities within the one systems phenomenon of the person as they do outside in society.

There is one final system that the proposal of Object Relation-Systems Theory has to offer as a new applied concept: the model of mutual deviation-amplifying systems. Let me give an example of this model with another crisis case. A Puerto Rican man, deeply depressed, comes in with a request for help. As good crisis interveners, the team seeks out the ecological givens that may have been precipitants to his crisis. They uncover the fact that because of the recent social and financial difficulties of the economy, he has been left without a job and forced to seek a new one. His current work brings home a salary that is enough to support himself, his wife, and two children but requires drastic changes in the family's style of life. His wife recently became very angry with him for not doing better. As family ecologists, the team became aware of the particular contributions which the present financial crisis was having on this subsystem and planned to hold a family session to help this man and woman deal with their triangulation, with their area's money plight, and with the resulting tensions that it was having in making them more angry with themselves. The team also moved to help them determine what alternatives, besides depression and anger, they might have to handle their crisis more productively.

As a member of the mini-team on this case, but one who was wearing the "goggles" of Object Relation-Systems Theory and not just of family-ecology theory, I saw some other interesting givens in this case in addition to the ones already mentioned. The man, for example, talked about how for as long as he could remember, he had often heard his father state that our client would never become as successful as he had been back in Puerto Rico. This was particularly difficult for him because he said that everyone in his family network was known to be financially well-off. Indeed, as the client talked, it became clearer that this was the unverbalized family agenda for everyone coming into the family (at least for all of the men). "The main job in life is to gain more than ordinary success." The more he talked, it seemed that the man was involved in a mutual deviation-amplifying system. Thus, a number of psychic introjects were relating to each other in a closed spiraling loop that was resulting in more and more deviation for the man from the norm of psychic organization and peace toward the deviation of disorganized psychic depression.

The diagrammed map would look something like this: The introjected father tells him that he cannot be as successful as he. The man is mildly depressed at this, but the family introject urges him to fulfill the family agenda to be a success. So our friend tries by getting a good job in New York City. Once he obtains it, his father introject reminds him that he can't do it, making him more depressed than before. This increased depression impedes his performance on the job, thus making him doubly depressed and prime target for his family introject to castigate him for not fulfilling its demands that any male member be successful. This, in turn, makes him triply depressed and more susceptible to the reprimands of his father's introject with resulting greater depression, etc., etc.

He is locked into a vicious circle of interacting internalized introjects that comprise a system which has as a basic result the continuing and spiraling amplification of his depressive deviation. This is obviously not simple linear cause-and-effect; it is, rather, an internalized system that amplifies deviation—in this case, the deviation of an unproductive depression. Subsequent analysis of the goings on in the person has convinced me that not only is there linear causality triangulation occurring in the person but also, mutual deviation, amplifying systemic causal reactions. But then, in a theory that takes in object relation plus systems, one should not expect anything different.

SOME POSSIBLE PSYCHIC ENTITIES OF OBJECT RELATION-SYSTEMS THEORY OF THE PERSON-SYSTEM

As only a beginning in the proposed concepts of this presentation of Object Relation-Systems theory, I would like to mention no more than four introjects. The first is probably the most complicated one. I choose to call it the mutually amplified intro-ject. You will recall my description of the causal system which is known as the mutual deviation-amplifying system. It has been called on to explain many systems phenomena in the sciences from an explanation of amplification processes in evolution itself to the amplification of so-called mental illnesses in whole societies. Let me alert you to this consideration—the deviation which is amplified can be judged either to be deviant or not but is not necessarily a deviant occurrence though it always is a devia-tion that is amplified. Now, in a mutual deviation-amplified intro-ject, a significant object is introjected and then, in its interactions with the other objects within the person, its original perceived state is altered and amplified until it ends up quite different than when it was originally introjected. Thus, an originally introjected angry parent can end up as being perceived in a much more angry-amplified way.

This mutual deviation-amplification process can also occur outside the individual in a way reminiscent of the introjects of which Melanie Klein spoke. For her, the person can project anger on an un-angry significant parent, for example, and then intro-ject the object as being angry though in the objective reality, this is not the case. In a somewhat similar process, I propose that a child can project outside of himself an introject onto his peer group system of siblings. Then, through mutual amplification by this peer system, the introject can be handed back with a deviation now amplified and reenter the person of the child as perceived with amplified properties not there before.

Triangulated introjects are the second type I would like to mention. Analytic Object Relation Theory always talks of single objects that are introjected by the person. Because triangles occur in the objective reality of society and are perceived through the phenomenology of the person, the theory of Object Relation-Systems must take into account as one of its tenets that triangles can be introjected not as three individual objects but as a triangu-lated unit or object. (I have a client whose intraperson is constant-ly taken up with an introjected triangle of a highly competitive and jealous husband-mother-brother, and this introjected triangle's constant interaction with her own central ego keeps resulting in many ongoing conflicts for her.)

The third introject is what I call the isomorphic introject. For a long time, we family therapists have been intrigued by a common phenomenon by which a person can end up with the traits of a person two generations removed in the family tree even though the client may never have met or for that matter have heard about that person. I, for example, recently discovered that my "sound of a different drummer" personality, the origins of which training analysis never was able to solve to my satisfaction, mirrors a great grandfather I never knew about. It has seemed to me that two possible ways of explaining this is that family members may have passed on these traits unconsciously or perhaps, in some presently unknown evolutionary genetic way. (Another far out possibility has always seemed to me that it may prove that the past person has just been reborn!) The most plausible explanation and most scientific, however, though also the most complicated, is that it is an example of what the system theoreticians call isomorphism: when two events take place which are mirror images of each other but are not so because of any connection between them. Through this systemic process, therefore, many people within family systems that I have observed have ended up with introjects of past generations which can only be rightly called isomorphic introjects. There can also be what I call "shared introjects" within the theory of Object Relation-Systems. A growing child can be given from his experiences with those on the outside, be they parents, significant adults, or peers, or siblings, these persons' own introjects and then borrowed, as it were, by the child as part of his or her own phenomenology.

The last introject to which I would like to allude at this time is what I shall call the network introject. We have recognized for some time that groups can, as groups, have their own unconscious, which is not a summed product of the individual unconsciousnesses of the parts of the group. Similarly, groups can also have group identities which are not the sum of the individuals who are members. The unconscious and conscious group-objects can be incorporated back into an individual and become an introject of that person and thereafter, belong to him or her as part of his or her objects.

These, then, are some of the concepts which may lead to a new formulation of the person on that system level in Object Relation-Systems Theory. I do not mean to say that this theory should replace analytic treatment or family ecology therapy. Both operate on different system levels, and both have their legitimate and valid goals as treatment modalities, and both, therefore, have their specific patterns to effect these goals. However, both need to wear each other's "goggles," and both need to have a unified theory of the person and family which can represent the total reality of the clients whom they are helping and healing. I do not suggest in any definitive way that this paper proposes what the theory will end up looking like. I have merely shared some possible concepts that I, as one who deals in both therapies and theoretical system levels, propose, concepts which can hopefully lead one day to what this theory may begin to look like.

BREAKING THE HOMEOSTATIC CYCLE

Lynn Hoffman

A virtue of family therapy is that it allows one to identify the sequences associated with irrational behavior in small social fields. Many family therapists have created personal vocabularies to describe the dynamics or the structure of these sequences. Bowen talks of a network of linked triangles in which twosomes are always changing partners.[1] Minuchin speaks of a child and his parents caught in "rigid triads" which may take a variety of forms.[2] Haley, who was one of the first to call attention to cross-generation coalitions as a sign of dysfunction in a system, is now advising clinicians to look for a triangle consisting of an overinvolved parent-child dyad and a more peripheral parent.[3]

The diversity of these descriptions conveys the dilemma of the art. How is one to know which pattern to look for, let alone identify, when one is in the presence of a strange family, peering into the gloom of its manifold transactions? Surely, there is a formulation which would operationalize triadic concepts so that one could say to oneself during a family interview: "There it is! That one there!"

Haley had spoken to this issue many years ago when he made a plea for a descriptive language for interaction that was not purely dyadic. For illustration, he chose a repetitive sequence in a family with a disruptive child.

> The child would misbehave in some way, for example, by leaning down and looking under the table. The father would speak to the child and tell him to straighten up. Mother would then speak to father and tell him that he should not have chastised the child at that time or in that way. Father would say he was merely reprimanding

the boy because it seemed necessary, and mother would look exasperated with him.[4]

Haley suggested that such a sequence might occur at a time when the family or a particular relationship in the family was threatened with change. The sequence, not just the misbehavior, served some kind of change-resistant or homeostatic function. Moreover, this kind of sequence did not represent causality in the usual sense; it was a cycle. Each person's behavior was influenced by the behavior of the other persons, who influenced their behaviors in turn. Getting one element to change would cause the other elements only to readjust so that the outcome would be the same.

Haley used this example as a take-off point for a model of the family as a cybernetic system, rather than staying with the program he described. What a pity! Even though this little piece of interaction seems nondescript, lacking the grandeur of a truly pathogenic display, it deserves attention. Haley had caught a sequence which child-oriented family therapists were to see or hear reported over and over again in their offices. It was a common example of a group of homeostatic cycles relating to the symptom of a child. When experienced family therapists find this cycle, they direct an intervention toward it with the precision of a laser beam.

If one could isolate and describe a few instances of cycles of this type, even if one could not exactly explain their dynamics, it would be a step toward achieving greater accuracy in making assessments and formulating interventions. This paper will not examine interaction cycles of every kind (couple cycles, for instance) but will concentrate on only this one type. Illustrations will be from interviews with families where a child is the problem and will be limited to those occasions when an experienced family therapist recognized this cycle and carefully interrupted it.

THE ANATOMY OF A CYCLE

Let us move to an example of such a cycle, a recurrent sequence which takes place between father and son in the interview "No Man's Land" in Haley and Hoffman's *Techniques of Family Therapy*.[5] The triangle consists of an ineffectively domineering father, a mildly rebellious adolescent son, and a mother who sides with the son. Father keeps getting into an argument with the son over smoking, which both mother and father say they disapprove of. However, mother will break into these escalating arguments to agree with the son, after which father will back down. Eventually, father does not even wait for her to come in; he backs down anyway. This sequence occurs several times, with variations, during the interview. To give some idea of the flavor, here is one of the shorter versions; the mother has already said that she is not in favor of taking away the boy's allowance:

> Mr. R: (to Mike) Would it please you, I presume it would, if I said that it was all right with me for you to smoke: Would that make you feel better?
>
> Mike: Yes, I guess it would.
>
> Mr. R: Well, for your sake, Mike, I wish I could, but I honestly and truly can't. I still don't think it is the right thing to do. (Pause) I really don't.
>
> Mike: Well, by taking my allowance away, you're, you're both, not being, I'm not able to buy cigarettes, or I'm not being, I'm not able to do anything. I can't go to the show, I can't . . . .
>
> Mr. R: Now, Mike, whenever you have come to me in the last two or three weeks and asked me for money for some specific thing, I have given it to you.
>
> Mike: Those things I had to do. (Pause)
>
> Mr. R: You're right. You're right.[6]

The cycle illustrated above is a version of a homeostatic mechanism which redirects tension away from some other area of the family. Here, this other area involves a parental conflict. If the parents began to struggle with each other more directly, their own relationship might be imperiled. One can see that the stakes are high in favor of some arrangement which will allow the parents to express their differences but which will limit these differences to the topic of the boy's behavior.

One term for this arrangement is the "mirror-image disagreement." Stanton and Schwartz, in their book, *The Mental Hospital*, found that when two authorities on a ward were in an unacknowledged struggle with one another, they would often begin to disagree over the management of a case.[7] One authority, a therapist, perhaps, would take a protective interest in a particular patient while the other, possibly a nurse, would become strict and even punitive. The patient would become progressively more agitated as the polarization of attitudes between the two staff members intensified. However, if they could be brought to settle their differences face-to-face, the patient's agitation would usually subside.

In a family, the mirror-image disagreement may be hidden beneath an appearance of concern for, or antagonism to, the symptomatic child, but a persistent effort to get each parent to expose his attitude toward the symptom will usually cause the disagreement to appear. Most therapy with a child entails an effort to uncover this disagreement if it is not obvious, to disengage the child from his part in it, and to refocus it as an issue between the parents. But any attempt to block or shift elements in the cycle in which the symptom is embedded will often have the same effect.

A question now arises. If one speaks of a homeostatic cycle, one should also be able to define the factors which are being monitored by this cycle. It is too general to say "tension between the parents" and let it go at that. Presumably, there are essential variables which the parents—or whatever executive dyad is operating—must maintain within certain limits if they are to function together successfully. What might such variables be? Let us make a few guesses.

A characteristic of families where there is trouble with a child is often an unusually tight pair bond. The source of this tightness may be a fear of abandonment or isolation on the part of the spouses or it may be something else, but whatever the reason, the spouses seldom actually separate, no matter how intensely they may say they want to. Given this situation, there would have to be some ways, some devices, for creating distance in an otherwise suffocating closeness. One is reminded of studies which have been done of cats in their natural surroundings. Cats seem to need well-defined spatial territories, and if they have conflicts over space, will solve them by allotting different time spans to a particular spot. Cat A will sit by the hearth in the morning while Cat B will enjoy it in the evening. Cats approaching each other at an intersection where two habitual cat-paths meet will sit some distance from the intersection and wait, apparently not looking at, or noticing, each other. At a certain point, one of the cats will casually walk through, and then, the other cat will follow suit. A cat invading the territory of another will be greeted by a ritualized aggression display by the home cat, which seems to monitor the boundary between them.

Although humans have different closeness-distance requirements than cats, the case of cats furnishes a valuable way to think about the predicament of an over-close couple. Clinicians are familiar with the array of mechanisms for distancing which couples use. One device is to maintain separate physical spaces: different bedrooms, sometimes even different houses. Spouses still close to their own families of origin often use their childhood home as a place to which to escape.

Another device would be temporal distancing as when a couple managed to arrange a work schedule so that one spouse works nights and the other days, or a working spouse comes home late and then, is exhausted or unavailable. Emotional distancing is a common term but can be made to apply specifically to the kind of behavior that people use in crowded elevators when their bodies are pressed physically together but eye contact or other communications are avoided. Spouses who are practised in this type of avoidance find it hard to look at each other while talking during a family session.

Another form of distancing which might better be called a modulator of both distancing and closeness is the periodic bicker. These recurrent conflicts are nearer to the agression displays one finds in animals than anything resembling a fight that solves a real issue. One key to whether or not such behaviors are true conflicts or simply part of a closeness-distance cycle is whether there is a "cut-off point"—a sudden cessation of hostilities that seems to be triggered off by some minimal cue or is simply due to the timing of the sequence itself. These constant bickerings seem to reconnect a pair after a period of withdrawal and despite their negative aspects, must still be construed as a kind of contact preliminary to a new distancing.

However, overclose couples are apt to be fearful of any show of conflict, perhaps because open expression of differences is such a threat to the pair bond. A relationship style, commonly associated with conflict-avoidant families, is one in which one spouse is apparently the dominant party and the other the submissive party (subject to an occasional "flip-flop"). Ravich, who has tested many couples with a train-game which allegedly differentiates between symmetrical versus dominant-submissive patterns (among others), comments on the tendency of dominant-submissive pairs to stay together in spite of what he describes as the most exquisite marital misery in his experience.[8] They will also resist any attempt to change their pattern, and if the therapist does introduce a change, they will often drop out of treatment.

Another striking characteristic of couples who have a dominant-submissive relationship is that they seem not only conflict-avoidant but to have more than their share of seriously disturbed children. Couples with a predominantly symmetrical relationship (meaning one where the partners are relatively equal) will be more likely to come into therapy for a marital problem than for a child problem unless that problem is the outcome of a separation crisis or divorce proceedings. Researchers studying families of hospitalized schizophrenics will time and again describe the marital axis as one in which one spouse seems apparently the controlling one and the other the one who complies. All of Lidz and Fleck's examples of what they termed "marital schism" and "marital skew" in families with schizophrenic children are characterized by marital relationships which are extremely unequal.[9] Many of the spouse relationships in the families of children with severe psychosomatic disorders studied by Minuchin's project in Philadelphia fall into the same category. The mechanism which makes this arrangement so ideal for masking conflict has been pointed out by Wild, *et al.*, who found that in their sample of families of hospitalized schizophrenics, fathers were rated "over-controlling" while mothers came out "amorphous." These behaviors have a mutual causal effect on each other. The authors noted that: "Mothers' vagueness increases the likelihood that fathers will take over and control situations, and fathers' arbitrary and often irrational style of control increases mothers' vagueness."[10]

An interesting speculation arises as to the function of a dominant-submissive relationship in the case of an overclose pair. Two points could be made. Bateson, for one, investigates the possibility that in many areas, including human relationships, complementary and symmetrical forms serve as control mechanisms for each other.[11] For instance, a couple where one spouse is extremely dependent on the other will rarely separate. The function of a symptom often seems to be to create such a dependency when a split threatens. At the same time, a move toward symmetry may counteract the strains generated by a dominance-submission cycle.

The other point has to do with the closeness-distance axis. Let us go back to experiments with cats. When a number of cats is placed in a small cage so that spatial or temporal distancers are not available, a process will quickly take place resulting in a very rigid status ladder. There will be a dominant cat, and the others will deploy themselves down the ladder until one gets to the bottom cat, a miserable, cringing creature who gets "picked on" by all the rest. This experiment suggests that a strongly complementary arrangement might act as a means of distancing in a situation where the degree of closeness is a vital issue. If a married couple were to adopt such an arrangement, this would allow maximum closeness while at the same time, the status differential created enough of a barrier to give the parties minimum breathing space. If this status differential were to surpass its given limits in either direction, the marriage tie or the well-being of one of the partners would probably be threatened. As we have said, a move toward more equality might end in a separation where a move toward greater inequality might provoke a severe symptomatic response. Bateson notes that the stressfulness of a relationship based on assertion and submission can sometimes be lightened by a shift to another kind of complementarity based on fostering and feebleness.[12]

But neither of these horrid possibilities needs to happen if a third party, usually a child, can be brought in to monitor both the overcloseness and the status difference which is so often associated with it. Couples who must paradoxically seek distance because they are so tightly stuck together are inordinately vulnerable to coalitions with others. A spouse who can use a friend, relative, or child as a major source of support will have the edge over one who cannot. Hence the life-or-death nature of loyalty issues in such families. However, a family is not a war, and coalitions tend to be constricted by rules operating in the interests of the larger unit. It is here that the type of cycle we have been describing comes in.

THE CHILD AS A MONITOR

In the light of the above thoughts, how can we understand the cycle featured in the "No Man's Land" interview? For one thing, the marital dyad seems to be mildly dominant-submissive with the husband trying to take an authoritarian stance toward his not-too-compliant wife. We find out that he maintains considerable emotional distance from her, a situation she reinforces by investing herself in other relationships like a girlfriend of whom the husband is jealous and, of course, the son. The wife's weaker position in the marital subsystem is counterbalanced by her strong position in the parental subsystem where she has a not-so-covert ally. The son's involvement is able to affect both the power difference in the marriage and the closeness-distance axis so that neither variable is driven too far from its usual limit.

What has apparently happened to upset the family balance is the advent of a major transition point: the adolescence of the son. He is entering a period where he can realistically challenge his father. On the other hand, the normal pulls of growing up tend to detach him from his mother and "female ways." It is logical that the behavior which brought the family to therapy was his breaking into a tobacco store and stealing cigarettes and some change. The action relates, also, to the major issue between the father and son: smoking.

In the repetitive argument over smoking, the problem the boy faces is the mirror-image disagreement between his parents. If he does not smoke (is *not* rebellious), he supports his father against his mother; if he does smoke (*is* rebellious), he supports his mother against his father. If this kind of interaction had been allowed to continue, the boy would probably have taken flight into another kind of behavior which would force his parents to unite in order to deal with him.

The therapist, Charles Fulweiler, seemed to know that this sequence was important to move in on. The methods he used were mostly blocking maneuvers, supported by interpretations. However, a part of his style is to enter and leave the room without warning. He took advantage of his entrance in order to inhibit the cycle we have described at strategic points and to turn it step by step toward a different direction. He used his first entrance to cue the mother to be more explicit in her defense of the son; the second entrance to pick out the disagreement between mother and father; the third entrance to back up the father's authority in the face of the mother-son combine; and the next two or three to stop the father from taking the role of victim while at the same time clarifying the mother's part in rendering the father ineffective. The interview ended with nobody to blame because all of these events had their roots in the past.

So much for the immediate intervention. Over the longer haul, which may mean anywhere from ten sessions to two years depending on therapist and family, it is best to prepare for the consequences of breaking this cycle. A disruptive child offers his behavior like sticky bait to the overinvolved parent (the father in this case), and the resultant conflict triggers the less involved parent (the mother) to step in. Here, the mother is able to make a coalition with the boy quite openly; if she had been more covert about it, one might have expected a more serious symptom. The overinvolved parent is usually the outsider in the triangle, and much of his inappropriate anger and in this instance, sense of helplessness and backing down, may come from this fact. In the closeness-distance area, the wife maintains the upper hand by having an affair to go to, so to speak. In this way, she can reverse the imbalance in their relationship while maintaining distance. But her husband, by exaggerating, even inviting, his own helplessness, uses the magic power of complementarity to "stick" them back together.

Obviously, if a therapist breaks this cycle, he has to help the couple both with the closeness-distance problem and the one-up/one-down problem so that they no longer need a third party as a monitor. Fulweiler made a beginning attempt in the first interview to alter both dimensions and apparently was successful because the boy stopped being perceived as a problem very soon, and the couple went on in therapy without him.

BREAKING THE CYCLE IN THE ROOM

Dr. Salvador Minuchin of the Philadelphia Child Guidance Clinic consciously attempts to revise relationships while the family is in the room. Inexperienced therapists watching Minuchin shift and restructure relationship patterns within two or three minutes of meeting a family for the first time are surprised. Minuchin will say that there is no need for surprise; he has seen this particular family constellation so many times that he needs only minimal cues to recognize it.

It is also possible that what Minuchin is talking about has to do with the cycles we have been trying to describe. He does not particularly emphasize cycles in his writing, but an examination of his therapy reveals that he is sensitively attuned to them. Let us take for an illustration the first few minutes of an interview with a family of a little girl of four, described by the parents as "uncontrollable." The session included the parents, Karen, the patient, her two-year-old sister, Laurie, the family's therapist, Dr. F., and Dr. Minuchin, who came in as a consultant. The father, who was a policeman, as usual wore his gun to the session.

Karen: Hi.

Dr. M: Hello. How are you?

Karen: Fine. Can we play with toys?

Dr. F: We're going to get some toys.

Dr. M: (to Karen, smiling) You said that your name is Karen?

Mr. K: Yeah.

Dr. M: Karen, what's the name of your sister?

Karen: Laurie.

Dr. M: Laurie? Hello, Laurie.

Karen: Don't pick her up. Don't pick her up. Don't pick her up. . . . Do you know why?

Dr. M: Why?

Karen: 'Cause she has a sore arm.

Dr. M: She has a what?

Karen: She has a sore arm because she fell out of her crib.

Dr. M: Which arm . . . this one or this one?

Karen: Which one, Mommy?

Mrs. K: The left one. Which one is that?

Karen: This one, right?

Mrs. K: Uh hm.

Karen: She cracked her, ah. . . .

Mrs. K: Collar bone.

Karen: Collar bone.

Dr. M: Oh my goodness!

Karen: It went ka-bam! And Aunt Dorothy . . . do you know why she fell out of the cri- she put, she fell out of her portacrib again.

Dr. M: (to parents) Let's share that, so we need to sit together.

Mr. K: Okay.

Dr. F: I asked Dr. Minuchin to join us because four eyes are better than two. Dr. Minuchin is director of the clinic here.

Karen: Is that mine?

Dr. M: No, that's mine. (She sits on a table.)

Mrs. K: Don't sit on the table, Karen. What is that?

Karen: That's the table.

Mrs. K: Okay. Don't sit on the table, Okay? You sit on chairs. Okay, honey?

Karen: Doc . . . doc . . . doc . . . doc . . . (continues to repeat this as she runs around the edge of the room, touching the backs of the chairs.)

Mrs. K: She seemed pretty wound up lately. I don't know whether it is Christmas or maybe. . . . No, Laurie, no sweetie.

Karen: Are there any toys?

Dr. F: Here are some toys.

Karen: I want to play with . . . here, Laurie, you play with the dragon.

Mr. K: (chuckling) Dragon.

Karen: Do you have any paper?

Mrs. K: Not today, sweetheart. No, put that back, we don't have any paper to draw on. Put them back Karen.
Karen, do what you were told.
Put them back.
(to Dr. M) Her belligerence is so. . . .

Dr. M: Is that how you run your life? Is that how Karen and you spend your time together?

Mrs. K: Yes . . . yes.

Dr. M: It takes just a minute-and-a-half to see it.

Mrs. K: Yeah. Like, it's a continuous battle.

Dr. M: Um hm.

Mrs. K: You know . . . at least for me.

Dr. M: Um hm. Who wins?

Mrs. K: It varies. If I'm (sigh) up to fighting with her, at that point, sometimes I do. You know, I leave her win sometimes too. You know . . . but we do try and get her to do what we say even if it is a fight. (to Mr. K) Don't we?

Mr. K: I make her.

Mrs. K: Yeah, right.

Dr. M: (to Mr. K) What was your answer?

Mr. K: I make her do it.

Mrs. K: Right.

Mr. K: I always win.

Karen: (in background) Doc . . . doc . . . doc . . . doc . . .

Dr. M: I feel there is a little difference.

Mrs. K: Yeah, there is.

Dr. M: (to Mr. K) You make her do it. . . .

Mr. K: Yeah, I make her do it.

Dr. M: . . . but she doesn't (indicating Mrs. K)

Mrs. K: No, not all the time . . . no.

Dr. M: Do you find this present arrangement a difficult one? For example, the two girls going around while we talk? How do you respond to that?

Mrs. K: How do I respond to it? I get tense.

Dr. M: You get tense?

Mrs. K: Yeah, I do get tense.

Dr. M: So, you would prefer that she stay in one place?

Mrs. K: No, I can see them walking around when there are toys for them to play with.

Dr. M: What would you like?

Mrs. K: Right now?

Dr. M: Yes. What would make it more comfortable for you?

Mrs. K: For them to sit over there and play with the puppets.

Dr. M: Okay. Do that. Make her do that.

Mrs. K: Karen, go over here and play with the puppets, okay? Go ahead. No, not here. No.

Karen: Why?

Mrs. K: Go over and play with the puppets.

Karen: I don't love you.

Mrs. K: I love you. Go ahead, go play with your puppets.

Karen: I don't want to play.

Mrs. K: Karen. . . .

Karen: Laurie's playing with them.

Mr. K: Karen, will you sit down?

Dr. M: Let mother do it. You know, she's the one who does it when you are not there.

Mr. K: Yeah, yeah.

Dr. M: So, let her do it.

The presenting problem in this family, like the other one dealt with in this paper, is disruptive behavior. The scenario which includes this behavior is, in the case of a young child, easily provoked into happening in the room. In fact, it usually occurs without prompting. Within a few minutes of the beginning of this interview, the mother is asking the child not to sit on the table, but instead of following up the order with action, asks her the name of the thing she is sitting on and again tells her to get off it because "you sit on chairs." The child does get off, but she does not sit on chairs; she begins to circle the room very noisily. Mother tries to make her behave, then turns to Minuchin, indicating how help-less she is.

Minuchin then ascertains that this is the way the child behaves at home and also, that the father is the only one who can make her obey. He suggests to the mother that she could ask her little girl to stop running around the room if she does not like it. Mother tries again, and when she does not succeed, father comes in as usual to establish law and order. Minuchin blocks father's helpful maneuver, telling him that as his wife has to contend with this behavior at home, she is the one who must control it now. Thus, the scenario which generally happens does not happen. The therapist has interrupted a cycle.

What follows this intervention is a suggestion to the mother which helps her to succeed in quieting the little girl down. Minuchin has her get down on the floor and play hand puppets with her. This is a positive rather than a negative reinforcement for behaving well and is an action rather than words. The mother plays for a bit, but soon her tendency to criticize takes over. Minuchin then invites the father to sit on the floor, and soon, he and the other therapist and Minuchin are also playing with the little girl. The therapist ends this sequence by commenting on the father's gentle way of playing with his daughter. By now, of course, she is behaving like an angel.

The session ends with Minuchin excusing the children and speaking with the parents. He discovers that the mother is afraid that when her husband intervenes to control the little girl, he may lose control and hurt her. Minuchin expresses surprise and asks why she thinks that this father, who has just been playing affec-tionately with his little girl, would be capable of such a thing. The mother says that once, ten years ago, her husband got angry and had a violent outburst. He did not hurt anybody, but it was a memorable occasion, and the mother has never forgotten it. The therapist questions whether this is still a possibility since in ten years the father has never had a similar outburst. He suggests that perhaps the mother has been fabricating a personality for her husband. The mother leaves the session with some doubts in her mind, and the father is obviously relieved to be free of the stigma of being a "monster."

Therapy went very well with this family. The father stopped bringing his gun to the sessions. In fact, whether this event was related or not, he eventually left the police force.

This cycle is a little different from the other one we looked at in at least one respect. The helpless wife and the authoritarian husband carry a flavor of a dominant-submissive arrangement. The child, as was true in the other situation, is overinvolved with one parent (mother in this case), who becomes so unable to control her that she has to bring in her husband. Because both father and daughter are billed as "monsters" who are able to terrorize mother, one can assume that mother feels in some way like an outsider to these two, and also, that she feels neglected by her husband. Her struggle with the little girl has the flavor of hitting out at a preferred rival. However, when the husband does come in to control the child, the mother turns on him and sides with the child. It is a neat switch, because by one move, she not only separates father and daughter but becomes daughter's protector against father. Now, it is father who is the outsider! But the child has been the weight who changes the balance of the two sides of the scale.

CONCLUSION

A question always arises when methods which circumscribe the therapeutic goal are presented: Will the symptom disappear only to come back later, or will some other complaint take its place? And what about all the other obvious problems which are floating around in the family which ought to be fixed? The answer is not easy unless one is a purist about change. There are some purists who say that growth and a better life for each person in the family is the goal of therapy. There are opposite purists who say that they have no interest in changing the structure of the family but only wish to relieve people of the pain they complained of when they came in. Actually, because therapy is as complex a construct as families are, few of these purists do what they say they believe in doing. Experienced "small-change" purists go after a shift which will make interconnecting shifts take place elsewhere in the family *if one watches their work*. Experienced growth purists are extremely concerned about a presenting complaint and use all kinds of maneuvers to remove it *if one watches their work*.

However, the merit of training therapists to think in a more circumscribed way is that it brings therapy a little closer to the ideal of a precision instrument. There is an analogy here to the advance in medicine which allowed specific cures to be devised for particular ailments. Until recently, and amazingly so, doctors used generalized practices like leaching, cupping, purging, bleeding, which not only were useless, but actually did harm, because all of these methods dehydrated people. Psychotherapy, including family therapy, is just emerging from a similar dark age in which one global technique after another has been applied indiscriminately across the board. Family therapy has pushed cathartic approaches (in which getting out anger, or grief, or long-held secrets, would supposedly cure all symptoms), better communication approaches (which would supposedly help any relationship in trouble), paradoxical approaches (which work best when a family is caught in rigid homeostatic constraints but were often applied to all families), and if all else failed, the ideal of self-actualization could be held up for family members to aspire to so that even if they continued to experience their symptoms, they would at least be more autonomous human beings.

However, the concept of a more parsimonious psychotherapy is a coming idea in mental health not just for economic reasons but because it is beginning to seem *possible*. The advantage of focusing on the homeostatic cycle which supports a symptom is that it speaks to this issue of parsimony. The therapist can ascertain the variable that is being maintained, isolate the part played in it by the symptom, and then seek out the most effective way to block the cycle, using the fewest possible moves with more effective family functioning.

FOOTNOTES

1. M. Bowen, "The Use of Family Theory in Clinical Practice," *Comprehensive Psychiatry* (1966), Vol. 7, pp. 345-374.
2. S. Minuchin, *Families and Family Therapy* (Cambridge, Mass., 1974).
3. J. Haley, "Strategic Therapy When a Child is Presented as the Problem," *The Journal of the American Academy of Child Psychiatry* (1973), Vol. 12, pp. 641-659.
4. J. Haley, *Strategies of Psychotherapy* (New York, 1963), p. 158.
5. J. Haley and L. Hoffman, *Techniques of Family Therapy* (New York, 1967).
6. *Ibid.*, p. 63.
7. A. H. Stanton and M. S. Schwartz, *The Mental Hospital* (New York, 1951), Chapter 15.
8. R. Ravich, *Predictable Pairing* (New York, 1974).
9. T. Lidz, *et al.*, "The Intrafamilial Environment of Schizophrenic Patients: Marital Schism and Marital Skew," *American Journal of Psychiatry* (1958), Vol. 28, pp. 764-776.
10. C. Wild, *et al.*, "Transactional Communication Disturbances in Families of Male Schizophrenics," *Family Process* (1975), Vol. 14, pp. 131-160.
11. G. Bateson, *Naven*, Stanford, California, 1967), "Epilogue, 1958."
12. *Ibid.*, p. 194.

PART THREE

SOME SPECIFIC TREATMENT CONSIDERATIONS

INTRODUCTION

Until recently, very few families came to therapy prepared to share the therapist's goal of exploring how the identified patient's presenting symptoms were a manifestation of family wide problems. When family therapists, a decade ago, introduced to the families of such individuals the concept of troubled *families* rather than troubled *individuals*, they were sometimes surprised to find that certain families were very ready, even eager, to shift to a family frame of reference and quickly immersed themselves in the family therapeutic endeavor. On the other hand, other families, perhaps the majority, continued "prejudicially to scapegoat" their "patient" and to have difficulties in adopting the goal of work with the family as a whole. For many families and some therapists, the adoption of a family orientation is especially difficult when conspicuous behavior and symptoms have emerged in one or another family member and have resulted in hospitalization, legal charges, school expulsion, foster placement, etc.—events that may dominate the presenting picture.

In these instances, the community as well as the therapist and the family are likely to focus, at least temporarily, upon the individual even when it is quite reasonable to infer that the symptomatic difficulties of the individual are a manifestation of more covert problems in the family as a whole. External circumstances may make family therapy impractical or "contraindicated" even when the same problem under other circumstances might be quite suitable for family therapy."[1]

Writers who have discussed indications and contraindications for family therapy have most often defined family therapy as the treatment of two or more family members *meeting conjointly*, at least during much of the therapy, and have considered a variety of specific indications in which conjoint family therapy seems preferable or not compared to other forms of psychotherapy.

The question is whether there are indeed particular conditions that respond more easily to family therapy than to other forms of treatment. Unfortunately, there is little or no systematic research that has actually compared alternative approaches with the same kinds of problems.[2]

In Part Three of this monograph, we have attempted to present four possible problem areas which might lend themselves to a family treatment approach. In this way, we hope to expand the content area so that systematic research assessments might be enhanced by these discussions.

It has been suggested on the basis of clinical impressions that the problems of adolescence involving separation from the family are examples of a condition for which family therapy is easily indicated (Ackerman, Wynne) although the use of individual psychotherapy for the adolescent, in addition to the family therapy, appears to be a commonly recommended combination (Jackson, Shapiro).[3]

Perhaps the most common, though vague, indication for family therapy is the failure of other forms of treatment. As treatment failures are especially common with schizophrenics and other psychotic patients, with alcoholics who must be involved in new life styles and the creation of supports for new patterns of behavior, with the biological families of the placed child who constitute the down-trodden of our society, the disinherited, the so-called hard core, it is not surprising that family therapy has been tried with these, among others.

The four papers of this part look precisely to these four problem areas and offer for consideration some in-depth family treatment interventions.

FOOTNOTES

1. The Committee on the Family Group for the Advancement of Psychiatry, *Treatment of Families in Conflict* (New York, 1970), p. 23.
2. *Ibid.*, p. 24.
3. *Ibid.*, p. 24.

ALCOHOLISM IN THE FAMILY SYSTEM

Celia Dulfano[1]

Successful treatment of alcoholism requires working toward goals more complex and far-reaching than helping the individual patient "sober up." True recovery involves a new life style and the creation of supports for new patterns of behavior. Consequently, the family of the alcoholic should be involved in therapy. The family system's transactional patterns which have been built around the patient's alcoholic behavior can be changed, and supportive patterns can be developed. Family therapy and other group methods of helping the alcoholic also bring into treatment a population greatly in need of mental health services: the spouses and children of alcoholics. Work with the family group can develop the family system as a healing and growth-supporting matrix for the entire family, not just for the index patient. The system properties of families with alcoholism are outlined, and treatment considerations are discussed.

In the past decade, great progress has been made in exploring and treating the problems of alcoholism. Alcoholism is now generally recognized as an illness which can be treated: laws passed by the Federal and State Governments protect the alcoholic and much has been done to educate the general public.

But unfortunately, most therapeutic efforts have focused on the individual alcoholic apart from his social contexts. In many cases, this focus is inadequate for recovery. Recovery goes well beyond helping the individual "sober up." It is nothing less than the development of a new life-style, a life-style in which new patterns of behavior achieved by the individual are supported by the individual's ecosystem.

Individual treatment helps the alcoholic achieve insight and

77

learn to use the psychic energy released when the drinking problem improves. Thus, sobriety can be attained. Recovery involves sustaining sobriety. To help the recovering alcoholic sustain his improvement, the clinician must work within significant segments of the client's environment.

In his study, "Falling Off the Wagon," Arnold M. Ludwig[2] reports that the reason alcoholics most often give for relapses is inability to deal with anxiety. Thirteen percent of his sample specifically blame inability to deal with anxiety in family life.

Alcoholism is sparked by family anxiety, and it, in turn, sparks family anxiety. As Bowen[3] has pointed out:

> . . . the symptom of excessive drinking occurs when family anxiety is high. The appearance of the symptom stirs even higher anxiety in those dependent on the one who drinks. The higher the anxiety, the more other family members react by anxiously doing more of what they were already doing. The process of drinking to relieve anxiety and increased family anxiety in response to drinking . . . becomes a chronic pattern.

Sustained recovery will depend on breaking this chronic pattern.

Furthermore, work with the family of an alcoholic brings into treatment a population desperately in need of mental health services. It is difficult to conceive of a more stressful and unhappy life than that which is affected by the aberrant behavior of an alcoholic. The alcoholic's frustration tolerance is low; his behavior is impulsive and inconsistent. His feelings of guilt, inadequacy, and worthlessness create a nightmare existence for him and those closest to him.

The pain of living with an alcoholic has been demonstrated in the many studies of alcoholics' wives. The classic theories describing women who marry weak men as aggressive and domineering have been sharply questioned by later studies. Edwards, et al.[4] conclude that wives of alcoholics

> . . . are women who have essentially normal personalities of different types, rather than of any one particular type. They may suffer personality dysfunction when their husbands are active alcoholics, but if their husbands become abstinent and the periods of abstinence increase, the wives experience less and less dysfunction. Concurrent with these personality fluctuations are changes in the wives' methods of coping with their husbands' drinking patterns and in the

roles the wives play within the family. In all of this, these women seem much like other women experiencing marital problems.

Alcoholism has tremendous impact also on children, even very young ones. Bailey,[5] for instance, feels that the most hurtful result of alcoholism is the distorted role models experienced by alcoholics' children, who may develop a skewed image of masculine and feminine behavior. In any case, it is not surprising that a high percentage of alcoholics come from alcoholic homes. There may, of course, be a hereditary factor, but the high incidence may also be due simply to the pathogenic effects of living with an alcoholic parent. Children who learn that alcohol is a method of response are in real danger of becoming alcoholics themselves or of, perhaps, marrying an alcoholic. Working with families with alcoholism can help repair such damage and prevent the next-generation effect.

THE STRUCTURE OF A FAMILY WITH AN ALCOHOLIC MEMBER

A family is a natural social group with a governing interactional structure which has developed over years of life in common. Exploring this structure elucidates the dynamics of individual members as well as the system properties of the group as a whole.

Minuchin's[6] paradigm of family structure presents the family as a system formed by the union of a couple. These partners bring their own ways of interacting to the marriage. Each has a set of expectations, recognized and unrecognized. These two sets will have to be reconciled in the process of family formation. The result of this process is the spouse system—a dyad with its own set of interactional rules, which are either compromises or areas of unreconciled differences.

When children are born, the spouse dyad must become a parental subsystem, incorporating new tasks. As the family develops, more tasks are added, and old ones phase out. The system adapts and changes. New transactional patterns must be developed, but the family also must maintain the continuity that ensures its members a stable reference group.

When we look at a family with alcoholism from this point of view, we see that alcoholism or its threat may have been present at all developmental stages, even pre-marriage. Each role definition made necessary by natural progression is affected by the necessity to adjust to alcoholism.[7]

In most cases, one of the traits typical of a family with alcoholism—denial—appears early. Typically, the alcoholic is seen as a "social drinker" who "gets a little high now and then, but never really drunk." Even when the problem has become clear, the alcoholic and his spouse are rarely prepared to face it, instead, the problem is hidden. Unresolved tensions develop, and the relationship deteriorates. The spouse subsystem's transactional patterns modify because of the need to cope with problem drinking without acknowledging it. Communications between the spouses become sparse, ridden with guilt and anger. Patterns for negotiating and resolving conflict may fail to develop because it is possible to blame all problems on one partner's alcoholism.

If the couple has children, the tasks of child-rearing fall largely to the nonalcoholic spouse, who tries to take on the roles of both parents in addition to the other family tasks. The alcoholic is pushed to the periphery of the family, and the guilt generated by drinking makes him participate actively in the process of excluding himself. His behavior helps cement an alliance of his spouse and children, who blame him for the family unhappiness. Any attempts on his part to re-enter will be regarded as intrusive.

The impoverishment of spouse subsystem transactions leads to overuse of the parental subsystem's communicational channels. As a result, the children become involved not only in the need to deny the problem of alcoholism but, also, in the transactions which ought to be bounded within the spouse subsystem.

The children group around the nonalcoholic parent. The oldest son becomes the substitute husband, or the oldest daughter picks up many of the mother's tasks. Middle children typically escape from the house. A smaller child remains the baby of the family even when well into his teens.

The older children's maturity helps stabilize the family, but this is a pseudo-maturity. If the alcoholic begins to "sober up," they begin to act out. Even children who are married and have children of their own may need to be brought into therapy when an alcoholic parent is improving in order to work through their childhood problems.

Alcoholism also affects the family's relationship with the extrafamilial. Even when the problems of alcoholism have become obvious within the family, the family hides them from the outside world. Sometimes, the family isolates itself from its social context just as the alcoholic isolates himself from the family. The family withdraws from the extended family, the church, and so on. Natural supports are foregone so that the secret can be kept. Or there may be a desperate struggle to keep up appearances. The nonalcoholic spouse becomes the family's representative to the world, and this further reinforces the overcentrality of this person's position within the family.

When the problem of alcoholism can no longer be hidden, the same defenses which the alcoholic presents in the family are presented to the extrafamilial world. Family members rationalize: "He had to drink because he is so tense." Or they project: "He had to drink socially for business reasons." Both patterns, of course, postpone a constructive approach to the problem.

By the time an alcoholic comes to treatment, these family defenses have been strengthened over the ten to fifteen years typically needed for the disease to become chronic. By this time, the family system is organized around the existence of a problem member. Sobriety, though longed for by the family members, can be a crisis which activates the family system's counterdeviation mechanisms.[8] If this crisis of sobriety is not dealt with in the family in the right ways at the right time, the alcoholic will not be able to rejoin the family as a fully functioning member.

TREATMENT CONSIDERATIONS

The causes of alcoholism and the way it intertwines with family transactional patterns have been elucidated by many investigators. But what can be done for this group of human beings—alcoholics and their families?

A therapist working with alcoholism must know its difficulties. The only way to learn what an alcoholic and his family go through is to work with the alcoholic patient. Then, it is possible to understand the point of view of the family which has had to cope with such stresses and to help family members accept the alcoholic back into the family system.

However, it is important to establish a therapeutic contract with the whole family before beginning work with the individual alcoholic. It must be understood that *the whole family will be seen in therapy, and the drinking problem will be dealt with.*

Sometimes treatment begins because the alcoholic has been

referred after a drinking bout. In such cases, family sessions should start as soon as the index patient is detoxified. The atmosphere of crisis is helpful: the family is ready to form any kind of contract that promises some help. In other cases, a family will come into treatment for "marital problems" or "problems with the children."[9] They have reached the stage where they must have help, but the habits of years hold. The therapist who picks up clues that a family in therapy is concealing a family member's alcoholism must help them face this problem in order to open it for therapeutic intervention.

If work with the individual alcoholic begins before a family contract has been set, it will be extremely difficult to get the family into therapy later. The family members are happy to relinquish their problem member into expert hands and not at all eager to explore their own limitations and the parts they play in reinforcing the drinking problem. And the alcoholic, who is necessarily receiving support from the therapist, is reluctant to let the therapist see him in a context where he is scapegoated and derogated.

It is best, then, to hold individual sessions with the alcoholic concurrently with early family sessions. In these individual sessions, the therapist can get a good history so that he can determine the state of alcoholism. Ego strengths in the alcoholic can be picked up and developed. Any small accomplishment is praised and reinforced to increase self-esteem. Close contact must be maintained—daily if necessary. It may be useful to set a daily time for the patient to call the therapist. This maintains communication and also begins the process of helping the alcoholic set a routine for his life.

Alcoholics Anonymous can be very useful here. The contact with people who have experienced what he is experiencing is invaluable to the patient as is the support of the group. Furthermore, AA can be continually available (as a therapist cannot be), and its members know how to deal with the crisis situations with which the patient does not yet know how to cope.

Individual sessions and the participation of AA make it possible to deemphasize the drinking problem in the family sessions. The family must learn to adjust to alcoholism as an illness, accepting it as they would any other chronic illness. Teaching the individual and family about alcoholism is a very important step. But they must also learn not to blame the alcoholism for all problems which arise. The interpersonal relationships which prevent the family from functioning as a healthy unit must be corrected, and family members must learn to grow as individuals.

One major target of family therapy will be the spouse subsystem. The therapist must work to improve communication and build trust between a couple who have suffered many years of hurt and dissatisfaction. They are accustomed to masking problems by blaming everything on the alcoholism. The therapist must block this way of avoiding issues and help the couple learn how to talk directly about their problems. Even when the alcoholic has been sober for some time, they will tend to revert to their previous patterns of avoiding; for example, "when you were drinking, I had to do all the housework. . . ."[10] The therapist can point out that this is a reappearance of the old patterns and make them deal with the conflict at hand.

Alcoholism has also been used as an excuse to mask sexual problems, perhaps ever since the beginning of the relationship. When the alcoholic partner begins to recover, neither partner knows where he or she stands. It is rare in the author's experience to find an alcoholic who is sleeping with his partner. Usually he is "on the couch,"[10] and one of the children may habitually share the mother's bed.

This is why a family often comes into therapy when the children begin to leave home. Up to this point, the nonalcoholic partner has been absorbed in the business of running the family. When the children leave, the gap cannot be filled by the impoverished marital relationship. Either the couple must become a couple again, or they must separate.

Much of the work with them can be done in couple therapy, but other modes of treatment also can be useful. The nonalcoholic partner can be seen individually for help in detaching from the drinking problem and finding the energy to create a fuller life. In general, he will have used the alcoholism as an excuse for not dealing with himself as a person. The author often works with spouses of alcoholics in group therapy, teaching them to cope with the problems of alcoholism and sobriety as they arise. It is important to help these people pursue some life of their own, and the alcoholic spouse must get used to the idea. Alanon may be useful in helping non-alcoholic spouses to develop the sense of growing as people without using alcoholism to avoid growth.

Work with the parental subsystem will center on helping the alcoholic reenter this subgroup. Mother and children are in coalition against him. The mother has taken over being both mother and father, and though she may resent the necessity, she will also resent the alcoholic's attempts to move back in. The therapist must help her make space for the father.[11] She can learn to consult her husband before answering a child's question, and so forth. In some cases, it may be useful to hold sessions with the father and children without the mother so that they can learn to interact without her mediation.

The children, also, must move to let father back in. Junior has been the man of the family. Now, he must move down a peg, back to being his parents' son. Often, he will have been the mainstay of his family. Now he may begin to act out. The therapist may have to help him to find compensation in other areas, particularly his peer group, to make up for what he is losing in the relationship with his mother. Groups like Alateen can help here.

CASE EXAMPLES

The alcoholic in the Bates family was the father, Peter. He had been hospitalized several times for different reasons, but he had never been treated specifically for alcoholism. In fact, he strongly denied having an alcohol problem. He had attempted suicide three times. His treatment consisted largely of tranquilizers, whose use he would inordinately increase when intoxicated. After his most recent suicide attempt, which he barely survived, he had been hospitalized for depression and tests to probe for brain damage.

When the family was brought into therapy, they maintained that the father was "functioning well," and they pointed out that he had maintained a good work record for thirty years though his company was now thinking of putting him on disability. However, if Peter contributed anything to a family discussion, the family would make a joke of it. Peter showed, also, a strong tendency to blame himself for anything wrong that happened. The mother was obviously the leader of the family.

The oldest child, Peter, Jr., was married and living away from the family. They were reluctant to discuss him and seemed to think of his leaving home as a betrayal. Susan, nineteen, Chris, fourteen, and Alexander, thirteen, lived with their parents. The parents did not share a bedroom. The mother indicated that she usually slept near the children's rooms because the father did abuse the children when he had had "a little too much to drink."

The caseworker picked up this clue and the physician's findings and guessed that this might actually be a case of alcoholism. In the second session, she confronted the family and won admission of the problem. A therapeutic contract covering family sessions and the drinking problem was agreed on.

Individual work with Peter began while he was still in the hospital. The therapist saw him daily, providing much support and encouragement. Peter's own father had been an alcoholic who rarely brought money home. He died when Peter was quite small. Peter quit school and began to work full time early in his teens. He had maintained an excellent work record, but he had always felt that his lack of education prevented him making anything of himself. In the individual sessions, aspects of his family of origin and his continuing relationship with his siblings were explored.

The therapist put Peter in touch with an AA chapter, and their work was of real help to him as he left the hospital. He needed their availability, and their approach was congenial to a man highly suspicious of psychotherapy. Their involvement made it possible to shove alcoholism aside during family sessions.

One of the major early family interventions was to confront Mary Bates with her habit of putting Peter down and ridiculing everything he did, particularly with the children. She was a very religious woman, one of thirteen children, and still closely involved with her siblings. She had married Peter thinking she could help him, but soon came to see him as selfish and pleasure-seeking. She was exhausted, and depressed, and introverted about her own problems.

The goals of the early family sessions, therefore, were to help Peter take more of a role in family affairs and get out of the doghouse, to help the family realize that their interactions played an important part in the alcoholic rages, and to help Mary relax. In conjoint family sessions, the father was encouraged to talk, and the therapist helped the family listen respectfully to him. Sessions were held with the children and Peter alone to encourage him to do things with them.

During this period, Peter had several relapses as is typical of some recovering alcoholics. These situations were shattering for the family, who began to feel that treatment was a lost cause. Therefore, the therapist had to teach them how to cope with relapses. They had to learn to react less violently, to help Peter get the medical treatment he needed, and not to close him out. It was important to show the family that Peter was trying hard, but sometimes things became too much for him. A therapist can work on both an individual and family level to help his clients integrate relapses as a positive experience in the acceptance of the patient's illness, and this was done in this family.

Before long, the two boys, especially Alexander, began to get closer to their father. This became obvious in family sessions when they began to address him directly and side with him. Mary recognized and respected this change, but when Susan began to solicit her father's support in arguments with her mother, problems arose. During one argument, Mary ordered Susan to leave the house. Peter came to his daughter's defense and called the therapist. Clearly, this was a crisis situation in which Peter's improved position as both father and husband was at stake. The therapist supported father and daughter but also helped them see that the mother, as part of a system in transition, also needed support. Peter was rallying, and Mary was being pushed aside. She needed someone to understand her difficulties. Peter was put in a totally unfamiliar position: he was being asked to support the partner who had always been the dominant, strong one. He was able to react with a great deal of understanding, and communication between the couple improved immensely.

Later in treatment, this family joined a multiple family therapy group with four other families. Serendipitously, Peter was the only father in the group. He had continued to improve but had not yet achieved full status as father and husband. Within the larger group, however, he began to emerge as a leader. The tendency of a multiple family therapy group to take on the configurations of a natural family system encouraged him to assume executive and parental functions within the group. All children tended to solicit his alliance, and he began to guide and direct them all.

The teamwork of the group's co-therapists was also helpful to Peter. The female co-therapist often took an aggressive stance, confronting Peter. Each time, the male co-therapist moved quickly to defend him and build up his position within the group. This provided a model of more competent behavior not only for Peter but also, for the others in the group, who also benefited from watching the therapists' problem-solving dyadic interactional techniques.

Working with the Bates family, the technical possibilities of using different subgroups were advantageously pursued. There were individual sessions with husband and wife. There were couple sessions, exploring the marital problems. There were sessions with the children alone, allowing them to verbalize their feelings toward their father which had hitherto been unexpressed. This allowed release of tension and inhibitions and consequently, freer exchange in family sessions. Finally, treatment spread beyond the boundaries of the individual family, and within the frame of the multiple family group, the Bateses found a wider opportunity to try out appropriate steps in adaptive behavior.

In this family, as in many others, initially there was great resistance. But the therapeutic contract made it clear that the entire family would be involved, and treatment goals were expressed in terms of the whole group. The focus was to help the system function, and good system functioning was defined as enhancing the well being of every family member, not just the father.

The alcoholic in the Giacomelli family was the mother, Anina. The family came into therapy after the father called a mental health center to request help for his wife who, he said, was suffering from a severe depression.

It is interesting to note that the structures of families with alcoholism tend to be similar whether the alcoholic is the mother or the father. The same coping and defensive mechanisms seem to develop and be maintained. It may be easier for a woman alcoholic and her family to hide her illness if she does not have a job to get to. But this advantage may be offset by the fact that she is expected to represent the family in school affairs, social events, and so on. In this case, the nuclear family lived very close to the extended family (as is not uncommon in families of Italian extraction), and the necessity to maintain a front within the neighborhood and the church dictated continual desperate lying and covering up. The patient herself believed that no one knew of her drinking. She disguised her frequent periods of incapacity as headaches, and everyone in her church sodality politely maintained this fiction.

In the first family session, however, the therapist who had picked up some clues that Anina might have a drinking problem, began to explore this possibility. The youngest child, Julian, aged eight, was the first to concede that his mother drank. Soon, the whole family was sharing their feelings about their mother's drinking. After the session, Mrs. Giacomelli got a quart of whiskey, drank most of it, and tried to cut her wrists. She had to be rushed to the emergency room. Therapy began again as soon as she was detoxified.

Again, subsystems were effectively utilized. Many sessions were held with the couple in order to explore their hitherto unacknowledged problems. The therapist encouraged Anina to confront her husband with his infidelity, and as this area was opened for discussion, she began to understand how her drinking, which had made her unavailable as a wife, had contributed to his search for extramarital warmth and companionship. Winning her husband back began to seem a direct reward for stopping drinking, and Anina set to work with determination. Soon, the couple was finding almost forgotten gratifications within their relationship, and the spouse subunit reunited.

Anina joined a group of women alcoholics. She felt uncomfortable with AA, but the therapy group gave her much help and support not only with her drinking problems but also, with building herself up in other areas.

Unfortunately, Anina's return to competence as a wife and mother forced her older children into a shattering role shift. The therapist tried to help them find compensations in other areas, but before much could be done, the oldest daughter, Carmela, eighteen, became pregnant. Though she was a senior in high school, she insisted on dropping out and marrying immediately. Unable to envision herself in any other role, she found it necessary to move immediately into the position of mother of a family of her own.

The family felt so disgraced that they decided to move to another city. Fortunately, Anina had built up enough strength to cope with all this, with the group's support. Therapy terminated when the Giacomellis moved, about eight months after initia-
tion.

In conclusion, it is reliably estimated that there are nine million alcoholics in the United States. Everything we can do to reach these individuals will help. But we must also be prepared to go beyond individual treatment to the index patients' family environments. Only thus can we change the environmental patterns which are encouraging the alcoholic to remain the family problem, and only thus can we reach the people each index patient is profoundly affecting.

FOOTNOTES

1. The author wishes to acknowledge the help of Frances Hitchcock in preparing this manuscript.

2. Arnold M. Ludwig, "On and Off the Wagon: Reasons for Drinking and Abstaining by Alcoholics," *Quarterly Journal of Studies on Alcohol*, Vol. 33 (1972), pp. 91-96.

3. Murray Bowen, "Alcoholism as Viewed Through Family Systems Theory and Family Psychotherapy," Paper presented at the Annual Meeting of the National Council of Alcoholism, April 3, 1973, Washington, D. C.

4. Patricia Edwards, Cheryl Harvey, and Paul C. Whitehead, "Wives of Alcoholics: A Critical Review and Analysis," *Quarterly Journal of Studies on Alcohol*, Vol. 34 (1973), p. 130.

5. Margaret B. Bailey, *Alcoholism and Family Casework* (New York, 1968).

6. Salvador Minuchin, *Families and Family Therapy: A Structural Approach* (Cambridge, Massachusetts, 1974).

7. Joan K. Jackson, "The Adjustment of the Family to the Crisis of Alcoholism," *Quarterly Journal of Studies in Alcohol*, Vol. 15 (1954), pp. 562-586.

8. Decompensation in the alcoholic's spouse may serve a homeostatic function in some family systems. Cf. Edwards, *et al.*, *op cit.*

9. Bowen, *op. cit.*

10. *Ibid.*

11. See also the chapter on the "Garcia family," S. Minuchin, *Families of the Slums: An Exploitation of Their Structure and Treatment* (New York, 1967).

OPENING MOVES IN CRISIS INTER VENTION WITH FAMILIES OF CHRONIC PSYCHOTICS

Susan K. Flinn
Lawrence O. Brown

The issue we are dealing with is that of applying a social systems view to the understanding of chronic psychosis, particularly schizophrenia, so that we might utilize institutional settings to provide alternatives to a hospitalization and to chronic hospitalizations. We have learned on the Family Service of the Bronx Psychiatric Center over the last four years of our program to widen and shift the focus of our work to the familial and social world that surrounds the identified patient (hereafter referred to as the I.P.) rather than to grapple with the individual chronic psychotic in his isolation, despair, and ambivalence. We have learned that that person is so caught up in, and reflective of, the dynamics of his family that therapy with him alone misses crucial factors in his past, present, and future life, and eventually sets up the therapist to feel as isolated and hopeless as the patient.

Let us start at the beginning of such work: A family brings an acutely psychotic member to the admissions office of a public mental health facility telling you of his previous hospitalizations for episodes like this one and asking you to hospitalize him again. The family members are feeling afraid, exhausted, ashamed, frustrated, bewildered, and hopeless, to name but a few of the emotions associated with reaching this point one more time. The family expresses that the I.P. is causing so many problems that they can no longer manage without the aid of some institution which they expect will work some change on their problematic member. They are, also, although not always explicitly, asking for relief and distance from the I.P. They make clear to you at the same time that the I.P. is obviously disruptive to the meeting or outstandingly deviant, that everything would be manageable if not for the problems he presents. One often hears the complaint, "See what I mean doctor; this goes on all night long." Assessment approaches which exclude the familial context and social setting, emphasizing a detailed evaluation of the individual's strengths and weaknesses in reality testing, judgement, memory, orientation, quality of thought, relatedness, and affective state will miss or underestimate the impact of contextual changes in the person's life. Even when present, the family is all too easily used as informants about the I.P. rather than understood as co-operators in a critical situation which is larger than any single individual. If we are stuck with the one-to-one model, then we tend to be overwhelmed when confronted with intense demands to institutionalize someone who actually seems to be inviting that disposition, and we are likely to hospitalize the I.P..

We want to explore a different way of entering situations like these which changes the criteria for the decision to hospitalize or not. What follows is the social systems view of chronic psychosis that we want to apply to that family clamoring for the admission of their I.P. to the hospital.

A fundamental assumption is that the symptomatic behavior of the psychotic person is not only an index of inner disturbance and distress but also, a signal that something has changed in his family or social network. This person is the least able to tolerate change yet expresses the results of change in his acute upset. For example, we often see that when a man retires, which leads to the need for a change in relationship with his wife regarding what might be characterized as his increased presence in her time and space domain, our chronic I.P. becomes floridly symptomatic. Another typical situation occurs when a parent must go to a hospital for medical treatment, surgery, or diagnostic testing. In the family of the chronic psychotic, this parent is rarely openly concerned about his own anticipatory stress but is usually quite vocal about the welfare of the I.P., who obligingly acts like a patient. Yet another situation involves the departure of the well-sibling for school, marriage, or job. The parents usually speak of the severity of the loss to the I.P. but never of their own sense of loss.

All of these situations are normal events in a family's life cycle. They require change and adjustment on the part of everyone in the family. The family of the chronic psychotic, however, usually attempts solution of these developmental crises by becoming more concerned about their patient and not by working at the real problem of change and loss. This displaced problem is more easily isolated and sent out of the family into the hospital. Since the I.P. cannot tolerate change and becomes symptomatic, he invites being labeled "mental patient" by acting crazy when his family is challenged and upset by the threat that change and loss represents to their rigid and precarious routines. The displaced problem (that is, from the original familial stress to that of a symptomatic member) is, then, easily isolated and extruded from the family into the hospital. His decompensation and symptomatic behavior creates an acceptable deflection of familial activity away from the painful issues of adjustment at hand and toward his turmoil.

We find that dealing with the actual change and how it affects everyone in the family, not just targeting in on the turmoil going on within the I.P., constitutes effective crisis intervention with families of chronic psychotics and is the very difficult opening phase in creating alternatives to hospitalization of the I.P.. In order to understand how these families came to have an I.P. in their midst, let us look at them over three generations.

Our experience leads us to see the development of the role of "career patient" in ways somewhat similar to Bowen (1965, 1960). We disagree with his view of the grandparents as mature and differentiated, as the grandparents we have had contact with have manifested dysfunctional behavior patterns which appear to be long-standing and would have to have interfered with their functions as spouses and parents.

Perhaps, there was some chronic difficulty between the spouses which was expressed in a distance between them, but it is not likely that these people stood out either as grossly pathological or as highly successful. One of their children, eventually to become the parent of our I.P., the least mature, remains more attached and involved in the relationship between the parents than other siblings. This person is often a concern to his parents, is perceived as needing special attention and comes to feel most functional only when involved in an over-close relationship which reproduces his relationship with the overclose parent. That relationship cannot be one in which differences between individuals are appreciated and integrated in productive ways. In fact, such a person is threatened by difference and newness and is usually reluctant to move out of his parent's protective orbit. His reluctance is supported by parental and sibling concern about whether he can make it on his own. When this person attempts to set up an independent life, he does so marginally with very tight connections to his parents. The world beyond the family is still somehow strange, alien, and not safe. When this person can move out sufficiently to manage the formal achievement of marriage, he enters into that relationship with a person who is also tied to her parents. People tend to marry others who have achieved similar levels of emotional maturity or who have reached similar degrees of differentiation from their families of origin (Bowen, 1965). This new spouse pair are both more invested in their parents than they are in each other. Each spouse always has the quality of a stranger to the other because the spouse is not part of that primary bond with the parents, inside of which is security. Out of intense need, somewhat rigid ways of relating to others, and inability to assimilate differentness, each of these spouses attempts to recreate that child-parent bond with each other.

Because each spouse is so infantile, neither can parent the other without feeling that he is giving up too much. They grow more and more distant over the mutual frustration of their infantile needs. In their daily interactions, the complexity of issues in their relationship and feelings almost never surface explicitly. Only one side of ambivalence becomes the overt language of the relationship. When they talk, their conversation is mutual in avoiding conflict or intimacy, exploring each other, or new ideas, or generating stimulation through variety. Instead, they tend to confirm what little they do agree on even if it is chronic enmity.

Regarding a wider social milieu, this couple is typically without friends and cut off from a full extended family so that when ordinary life problems crop up, they have no information about how others manage to handle similar problems. Their extremely constricted social background and current social network foster their lack of role flexibility and their inability to search for alternatives in solving problem situations. These people live an isolated existence with their only significant contacts being their own parents. Consequently, difficult life episodes are managed poorly as they have little resources for making adequate changes in relation to stress.

When this spouse pair has children, the process described for grandparents and parents is intensified. As each of these parents was special to his or her parents, now one of *their* children is singled out for special treatment—often because of some quality or trait which seems to call for such treatment. For example, the child may seem slow, be prone to illnesses, or perhaps, present some difficulties because of an organic or constitutional deficit.*

In any case, the quality of the relationship begins with, and is permeated by, a view of the child as unusual, setting the stage for an interaction between real or imagined characteristics of the child and the response of the significant others in his environment. It is in this interactional space that so much room exists for projective processes. This view of the child organizes the distant spouse relationship around the parenting function. The spouses' major area of agreement is to focus on the child's special needs, giving the appearance of togetherness. The parents' absorption in the difficulties of raising this child becomes the only constant emotional bridge between them. As the mother is usually most involved in caretaking, she becomes overly-close with the child or fused with the child in that she "knows" (but actually projects) his feelings and needs. In this fusion, she reproduces the bond of specialness which she had with her own parents.

In the recent history of psychiatry, we were blaming the schizophrenogenic mother for the child's pathology. We see now that father and mother, distant as spouses and viable only as parents, need the child and his problems to cement the marriage. The child presents problems and by doing so, keeps the marriage together on a parenting (not spouse) level for his own security. The child is, in effect, a caretaker for his parents and their relationship. There is no executive leadership on the parents' part; the family has no experience of a generational hierarchy, and we, as observers, feel confused. Because no one is in charge, it appears that the generational boundaries which structure most families don't exist here. With neither structural differentiation between generations nor executive leadership, no one is in charge of communicational traffic or rules of behavior. There is little clarity in family discussions because content is always at issue, never process. (For example, when a child interrupts a parent habitually, the parent habitually responds to what is said—not the fact that the child is interrupting.)

Returning to the development of the family under consideration, this triangular knot tightens, and we now have a child

---

*We want to make clear here that we have no quarrel with a biologically predisposed view of psychosis. The work of Rosenthal and Kety (1968) points dramatically to the likelihood that genetic factors play a significant part in the etiology of psychosis.

who is not going to be able to leave home because, in a real sense, he is a self only in connection with his parents. In addition, "outside" the family is an alien world. We cannot emphasize enough that this family is steeped in a tradition of isolation and apprehension of the world outside its doors. We have made home visits to people in apartment buildings where many tenants, like our families, have held the same apartment for upwards of ten years. The building seems friendly, with a sense of community. Our family reports never having a guest in the apartment or being a guest of anyone else. (By contrast, the family that produces children who grow to differentiate as separate individuals usually encourage and welcome a wide range of contact with friends, extended family, community, and exploration of new ideas).

A major thread of organization running through the confusion of the family of the chronic psychotic is the agreement between the parents to focus all energy on the child and not on the relationship between themselves. By the time we see these families, the child is so disruptive that we do not stop to consider that there is anything besides the child that is dysfunctional in the family, and by going along with the focus on the pathology of the I.P., we collude in the process called family scapegoating. Scapegoating may take various forms such as blaming or protecting, but its immediate and major outcome is to focus all the family's energies on "the sick one" and not on any other problematic situation. It's most common expression, put succinctly is, "We could be so happy if not for him," or, "Of course we'd like to go out to eat and see a movie together, but we can't leave him alone." Scapegoating is probably the most difficult pattern of interaction to change in families of psychotics.

To summarize, the social system of the chronic psychotic's family is one of emotional divorce between spouses who choose a special child to be unusually concerned with and whose specialness will mask their emotional divorce. The child's special function facilitates the blurring of the generational boundaries so that no one person or alliance between persons is clearly in charge at any given time. The process of scapegoating provides for a pseudo-mutual togetherness between the parents—a must for the insecure child who cannot tolerate changes in the parental relationship. These families are extremely isolated; they are without peers, friends, full extended family, and are unable to assimilate or accommodate to the external world.

This is a very broadly drawn and perhaps oversimplified summary of the key features of the development of the family in which we find a chronic psychotic. Against this schematic background, we must highlight inevitable evolutionary processes in the family in order to understand (1) certain aspects of the emergence of the psychotic episode and (2) how further episodes ensure a career of recycling through public mental health hospitals.

The most obvious feature of development, whether individual or familial, is the occurrence of change. The most outstanding feature of the representative psychotic family we have described is their inability to negotiate any change and separation. Change and separation present problems in adjustment for all of us, but because these families are so isolated and lacking in social resources, the stress becomes contained and amplified as if in an echo chamber. Most people have networks large and varied enough to help by providing support, innovations, or to run interference where needed and provide other points of view when change produces stress. The family of the chronic psychotic has very little or none of this kind of cushioning to help diffuse the stress produced by change. These families are often, therefore, highly rigid in their attempts to cope with change. Because their old and inflexible responses are not adequate for dealing with novelty, the change remains stressful. The responses to the continuing stress produce only more stress which eventually takes expression as a frank psychotic episode in the I.P..

Consider that typically, three generations within a family are alive and moving through the life cycle. This involves a fair number of people across a wide age spectrum, all operating in each other's orbits. They have no choice but to deal with births, deaths, marriages, illnesses, involvements with schools, courting, changes in job status, and moves to another location. For the most part, the path to chronic psychosis begins with the scapegoated child's first attempts to separate from or change his role within the nuclear family (which is one reason why the incidence of acute schizophrenic episodes is so high during the adolescent years). The cultural expectations and pressures to find a friend, to make it in a peer group, to begin to develop skills in relating sexually, or to establish some new role in a social system other than the family typically leads to the first acute break. Those pressures exist in sharp conflict with the fusion within the family, which doesn't allow the child to accomplish this normative shift from the family to another group. The child must remain the special problem of the parents, and the psychotic break further confirms for them their need to parent him. As long as this continues, the parents do not have to confront their spouseness in an empty home. Though we do not usually deal with first psychotic breaks in our agency, we think that the fate of that episode is determined by two gross factors: (1) the level of differentiation that person has attained (for example, how far out of the nuclear family he has been able to go before the break such as having friends and managing well with work or school), and (2) whether or not that first break is seen as a major life crisis and treated as a most difficult growth experience rather than as an introduction to the stigmatizing career of mental patient. First breaks seem to be best treated in a different manner from the repetitive decompensations characteristic of the chronic psychotic (Guttman, 1973 and Mosher, 1972). The families we are treating are ones in which that first episode of acute decompensation helped only to step up an ongoing scapegoating process by the assignment of a psychiatric diagnosis which validated and made official the role of scapegoat. By participating in this common flow of events, as we have all done, the mental health establishment joins the parents in affirming a career of specialness through deviancy for this child. It is for these reasons that we state frankly our belief that a psychiatric hospitalization, whether at this point or at a later point in the case of the chronic psychotic, is a most radical move. The result of such a disposition is that the family no longer has a difficult son or brother; the neighborhood no longer has a somewhat noticeable citizen; the school, no student: these basic social units now have a mental patient in their midst. The family's already skilled and responsive early warning system is now even more alert to watch for signs of deviance, which precludes more than ever the spouses' dealing with issues in their own relationship. Their vigilance increases the likelihood of finding such signs of deviance because of the scapegoating process, which in turn, increases the frequency of use of a mental institution to sidestep other familial problems which the I.P. is especially sensitive to and scapegoated for. As this tragic process recycles again and again, this isolated family, in their shame and guilt, retreats from whatever marginal network they may have had.

Our goal at this point is to stop the recycling. How can we, as therapists, set the stage for a family in crisis to think of alternatives to hospitalization when they have so often been relieved by having their I.P. admitted? Before walking into the room with the family, it is important to keep in mind that you need not hospitalize someone simply because the family demands it and because the patient is obviously severely disturbed. With that kind of orientation, you already begin redefining your role from that of "admitting personnel" to one of "problem solver." This does not rule out the possibility of hospitalization but puts it alongside other options. The assumption that we have painfully learned to make over the years is that the demand for hospitalization means that there has been some change, or that a change is anticipated somewhere in the family system, and that the whole family is in pain over this change. If we can figure out a way to decrease the pain quickly, the I.P., as the family barometer, remarkably improves, sometimes within the hour, but usually within a few days to a week. This assumption leads to a strategy for intervention the basic principles of which follow. We address ourselves to the first few hours of the encounter between patient and hospital when the situation is fluid enough to present some opportunities for avoiding automatic institutionalization. The goal of the intervention is to maximize those familial subsystems and dynamics which are sufficiently intact so as to keep the I.P. in the family while everyone works in a slightly different way toward the resolution of current stresses. The following points represent a posture to assume in the opening moves of this initial encounter. (For case illustrations covering a larger time frame, see Beels, 1975 and Langsley & Kaplan, 1968).

1. The family and others involved in the I.P.'s life are critical to the process, the outcome of which is the decision to hospitalize or to initiate other treatment tactics which fall under the general strategy of family crisis intervention. This cannot occur without certain preparations. When the I.P. arrives seeking admission unaccompanied by significant others, every effort must be made to bring in at least some members of his family network, friends, representatives of other helping agencies involved in his life, and the individual(s) with whom he is having the most difficulty. This should be done by concentrating on telephoning these people prior to, but as part of, beginning the helping contact. This sometimes laborious procedure is conducted with the explicit message to all concerned that no decisions can be made without their participation. This already begins to shift the expectations that some type of work will be done on, for, or to the I.P. alone to a situation in which everyone will have to participate in problem-solving.

2. Take charge of the meeting. In doing this, keep in mind that

you are going to have to generate a great deal of trust quickly, so be respectful of and try to join each person in the meeting. The family is usually upset and in an uproar, so your competence, refusal to be buffeted by the flap, and control of the meeting sets a tone conveying that you expect some productive work to be accomplished. Taking charge is a complex matter. It means becoming something of a conductor of a dissonant orchestra and creating a sensible flow out of the uproar. For example, slow things down if it is hard to follow someone; or stop members of the family when they interrupt each other; ask for further clarification of fuzzy statements. Only one person should speak at a time. You show that you are concerned enough to get a very clear picture of what is happening to everybody, which leads to the next point:

3. Listen to each member of the family including the I.P., thereby demonstrating that you expect he can be controlled and that he also has important information about the situation to contribute. Find out what each person is there for, and show each person you understand that he is in pain. This is one lever you might use to shift the atmosphere from a scapegoating session of the I.P. to a family focused meeting, that is, getting across the idea that when things change, everyone in the family hurts: Allow each person to ventilate without encouraging the amplification of feelings of anger, guilt, bitterness, failure, and the like. The intensifying expression of such feeling usually begins another round of scapegoating and antagonism.

4. Keep moving toward an organization of information that will help you to identify changes and point to possible interventions. What we have found extremely helpful in this regard is to draw, with the family, a map of their current life space in the style of a family tree. This map must include, also, any other important persons who are functionally connected with, but unrelated to, the family such as clergymen, representatives of other helping agencies, attorneys, school personnel, etc. This map, which we call a genogram, rapidly synthesizes a tremendous quantity of factual information in a graphic, concrete way. If drawn with ages and dates included, it allows us to see the family's social system in a large time frame from a perspective which can be very helpful in relating one event to another, which is often not apparent when taking a linear history. The map of their life space, used as a task, is useful on another level: it is the first activity on which the therapist and the family can work together which organizes the proceedings under the therapist's control. Our experience has been that it is often a major factor in leading a family to the experience of coordinated and productive interchange with a focus other than on the scapegoat. What often becomes apparent to the family are the relationships between episodes of decompensation and their own developmental crises

such as births, deaths, marriages, divorces, moves to new neighborhoods, anniversary dates, etc.. The genogram is the first tool one can use in making the current psychotic episode potentially understandable to the family by showing how the upset is a direct reaction to a change in their midst. As an open and shared reference document, the therapist can use the genogram to check out all parts of the social space and be thorough in identifying caretakers in the family and their state of distance, closeness, health, and so forth. Often a burdened caretaker's signal that he is overwhelmed is the change that induces crisis.

5. Demystify the symptomatic behavior, and keep moving in the direction of curtailing the family's scapegoating by translating the symptoms into terms that everyone can understand and relate to. Translate the symptoms as real reactions to stress in the family over an identifiable change. For example: "Mrs. Smith, now that your daughter has moved to California, you have been getting migraines, and your son has been hearing voices. You are both upset and show it in different ways." We might also call this steady effort a reframing tactic, the general style of which fits in with the next point:

6. Be supportive. Blaming makes things worse. Let the family know that they have worked hard on trying to figure out their problems up to now and that you appreciate their disappointment in finding that their best efforts have brought no relief. This allows you to shift to a problem-solving orientation with all of the family. Find out what they have tried already so you will know what did not work. Sometimes, you can introduce slight changes in a family's natural attempt to solve a problem in such a way as to make it effective under your new direction. The closer you stay to a family's style of problem-sovling, the easier it is to get them to attempt what you suggest. Once you cast the focus of the proceedings onto problem-solving, you can start to make moves in the direction of alternatives to hospitalization. The therapist's attitude of "Let's explore this situation together" shifts the pressure of "You must admit him" to a more plastic one. You are systematically lowering the intensity of the family's rage and helplessness so that the urge to expel the I.P. lessens.

7. Intervene very concretely and try to bring about one change. Do one thing at a time. You are trying to arrange an experience of success for this family, some sense of relief, and set the stage for further intervention to stabilize a very difficult situation simultaneously. So in designing a task for everyone to be a part of, be simple, and place the lightest burden of immediate change on the I.P.

8. Arrange for immediate follow-up, and give careful thought to where you want that to occur. In such situations, control is often tenuous and certainly organized around your efforts and presence. Have the next meeting on the following day if possible. In terms of

where that meeting takes place, we've almost consistently learned critical information or have done a very fine tuning-in to the familial style by making a home visit during the crisis phase.

9. When with families of chronic psychotics, try to work with a co-therapist. This is very difficult work, and one person can easily become rapidly enmeshed in the family, exhausted, and then give up. Keep in touch with your co-therapist when you are unsure about what is happening in the session. Feel free to talk with one another during the session in front of the family. Because time is of the essence, have pre-planning and post-sessions together so that you and your co-therapist can monitor how you are doing and shift strategies if necessary.

10. Interventions in situations involving psychotic behavior very frequently require the use of anti-psychotic medications. If one of the co-therapists is not a psychiatrist, who can prescribe medication, then, as part of their work preparatory to the meeting, the co-therapists must be ready to consult with an available psychiatrist who is sympathetic to crisis intervention as a modality of treatment and understands the same systems-language in which the co-therapists think. He must also be willing to follow the situation as it evolves with and through the co-therapists as they stay with the changing familial scene as the intervention proceeds over days or weeks. In decisions regarding medication, it is also helpful to ask the I.P. and his family about medications thah have been effective in the past. This facilitates the tactic of promoting everyone's worth as a helper and problem-solver.

11. A long range goal in working with chronically psychotic people and their families is to connect them up with a larger network of similar people who live in their neighborhood—in essence, forming a community within a community of people who continually turn to a hospital when they face change. By reducing their isolation, we reduce the risk of a future crisis. Successful execution requires continuity of care after the crisis has abated. We have found that families who are placed in multiple family groups after the crisis has ended have far fewer decompensations when faced with change than they had before being in the group and fewer applications for admission than families who are treated just during the crisis.

REFERENCES

Beels, C.C., "Family and Social Management of Schizophrenia, *Schizophrenia Bulletin* (1975), 13, pp. 97-118.

Bowen, M., "Family Psychotherapy with Schizophrenia in the Hospital and in Private Practice," in Boszormenyi-Nagy, I., and Framo, J. (eds.), *Intensive Family Therapy* (New York, 1965), pp. 213-243.

Bowen, M., "A Family Concept of Schizophrenia," in Jackson, D. (ed.), *The Etiology of Schizophrenia* (New York, 1960), pp. 345-372.

Guttman, H.A., "A Contraindication for Family Therapy: The Prepsychotic or Postpsychotic Young Adult and His Parents," *Archives of General Psychiatry* (1973), 29, pp. 352-355.

Langsley, D.G. and Kaplan, D.M., *"The Treatment of Families in Crisis"* (New York, 1968).

Mosher, L.R., "A Research Design to Evaluate a Psychosocial Treatment of Schizophrenia, *Hospital and Community Psychiatry* (1972), 23, 229-234.

Rosenthal, D. and Kety, S.S. (eds.), *The Transmission of Schizophrenia* (New York, 1968).

THE RESOLUTION OF THE
ADOLESCENT PARADOX
THROUGH FAMILY TREATMENT

John J. McCarthy

As a modality of treatment, family therapy has developed
through an evolutionary process which progressed from the
identification of illnesses in the patient to viewing the relationship
with the mother and the patient, to the realization that the father
and the "well" siblings shared in the psychopathology.[1] Yet it is
paradoxical that psychoanalysis, having recognized the enormous significance of early experiences for personality development and human behavior and the impact of the entire gamut of
dynamic interrelationships within the family, never sought to
involve the whole family in treatment.

In this paper, we are considering family treatment as a resolution of a particular behavior problem of an adolescent, viewing
the adolescent's pain not just as an adjustment to a particular
phase of growth, physical or emotional, but rather, as a symptom
of a disordered family system. Recognizing that there is disagreement among clinicians regarding the use of family therapy with
adolescents, we choose to agree with Minuchin (1971), Brown
(1970), Williams (1968), and Wynne (1965), who have discussed
the use of family therapy with the neurotically disturbed adolescent. Thus, we are proposing sessions in which all of the family
members including the particular adolescent are present in the
same room and are seen together by one therapist or multiple
therapists. We are further proposing that these sessions may be
structured for the sole purpose of clarifying the assessment, or
they may occur together with other treatment modalities such as
marital therapy for the parents or individual and/or group
therapy for the adolescent, or they may be the sole means of

treatment, lasting for a short or longer period to be determined by the focus of the particular interventive strategy.

Just as there seems to be definite indications when such family therapy may be a viable treatment modality, there are also strong counter-indications for the use of such a treatment process. Therefore, to cover adequately the theme of this paper, a summary of such counter-indications will be presented in the final section.

THE PARADOX

Self-identity and independence are the adolescent's major thrusts. He seeks to be himself, to personalize his own functioning. He is continually attempting to move away from close familial ties, to break the bonds. When we in turn are maintaining that family treatment is a valid modality for such a period of struggle, are we not setting up a contradiction in so many terms? Are we not truly promoting an even greater symbiosis?

There are many professionals who feel that the only answer is the highly confidential one-to-one relationship with a therapist outside of the family structure. They treat adolescents in a vacuum, preferring to function without ever touching the family system as such. Though they manifest skill in working with adults, they cannot treat adolescents within the family milieu.

In my experience, the end result is many times fruitless. No matter what the corrective relationship may be, it always comes under direct fire from the familial resistances. Seeing the adolescent together with the family members reveals what these resistances are and helps to reduce them to a level where they may be properly handled. The rallying cry of family members, whose homeostasis is threatened, is very real. It must be heard; it must be understood if any true adolescent individualization is to be accomplished.

The dyadic approach of adolescent and therapist has its place, but it cannot stand alone. And when the family pain is especially manifested through the scapegoated adolescent, that pain and its relation to the teenager must be brought out into the open. Delusions arise when the dyadic approach is set as the only approach. The family sabotage which takes place is very real, most of all when it is totally hidden.

THE ADOLESCENT CONFLICT

What are some of those major conflicts within the individual adolescent in relation to his parents which we first need to consider before we turn to family interviewing itself?

"Adolescence is generally described as a critical phase in growth, a period when there is eruption into consciousness of the unresolved problems of earlier phases of development. It is a time of physiological changes, of preoccupation with one's body and physical attributes, and of an emerging sex drive."[2] The process of adolescence does not move steadily forward. In this stage of growth, he vacillates between being a child and being an adult. He is often in a state of conflict, consciously desiring independence, unconsciously still needing to be dependent upon his family. "His inner turmoil manifests itself in erratic social behavior, in mood swings, in vacillating moral standards, in poor impulse control, and in shifting concepts of himself and the world around him."[3]

Ackerman emphasizes adolescent behavior as "ever-changing. It is unstable, elusive and evanescent; its true meaning occasionally escapes even the most astute observer."[4] Under these physical, psychological, and social stresses, adjustments which were accomplished during childhood need a total reorganization. It often seems that adolescence is a kind of second birth.

With the development of puberty, there arise strong genital strivings which the adolescents tries to deny because there is a regression to the phallic phase of development. When comparisons are made with older people, they find themselves grossly deficient. Often, the arousal of strong hetero- and homosexual erotization recalls the original parent-child relationship and with much guilt, they seek to push away from the parents. I have often been struck by the strong incestuous fantasies which linger in the shadows of associative story-telling, a startling dream, or pen-and-pencil sketches. Parents themselves have shared with me the erotic thoughts and feelings which they felt when even touched by a teenage son or daughter. These repressed desires and conflicts heighten a battle which sometimes leads to the adolescent's early separation from bed and board.[5]

The shared secrets and feelings of childhood quickly evanesce, and parents speak of being "hurt" because their children no longer share things with them. The expression of feelings seems to dry up. Others now share these feelings, generally members of a peer group, and parents resent this transitional stage. They find these friends uncouth, suspicious, and untrustworthy. After the initial maternal-infant symbiosis, and parental pre-school and early school closeness, it is a different world for parents, and they don't like it. Their own reaction is two-fold. Either they pull away in a reactive hostility, or they set up a symbiotic demand which carries with it a "mutual survival pact."

The adolescent turmoil is of such a nature that there is almost a disintegration of ego functioning and defenses. It takes months, even years, for new defense mechanisms to be set. They fight to become mature, but at times, there is a premature adoption of such a role, and the turmoil of conflicts going on within them is handled by outright denial. The end result is a created conflict with their parents. Thus, they want to be mature but are not, and they react with strong aggression against their parents.

During the initial phase of adolescence, the superego is under great stress. In childhood, there has been the introjection of parental values, standards, and morals. Now, these are being challenged by the ego, and the end result is guilt, anxiety, and depression together with severe yet ambivalent challenges to the parents' standards. Also, the ego-ideal, which is a remnant of the superego, becomes fragmented. The idealized identification with the parents is severely threatened. Other ego-ideals arise, those of friends, teachers, and the like. Parents are no longer the heroes of their children's world.

With all of these changes, the parents themselves react strongly. There results what I call the "primary rebellion" of the parents against their own sons and daughters. They rebel against biological, psychological, and social phenomena they don't understand, and they heighten this by failing to remember what adolescence meant to them. They become *laudatores temporis acti*, the extollers of their own past history. The reaction is certain: they are confronted with their adolescent's rebellion. But to me, this classical rebellion is always a reaction provoked by the primary rebellion of the parents and basic nonacceptance of the adolescent's ways. Where there is a parent's basic understanding, love, and acceptance, the storm can be weathered. It is a time of crisis, and adolescents need the parents' protection and good common sense. It takes a consummate diplomat to carry it off. Finally, an adolescent can be just as rebellious in accepting the primary rebellion of the parents as he can be in confronting it. Subservience manifested in the "good boy" syndrome may cloak deep hostility and anger and be signaled by somatic complaints, a lack of spontaneity or the presence of certain superego upheavals noted in obsessive-compulsive patterns of behavior.

My practice often leads me to explore the double messages of parents, their conscious and expressed wishes and demands versus the unconscious and subtly vicarious desires hidden within them. For the adolescent, it is like fighting a battle on two fronts. And often they die on two fronts trying to fulfill these wishes, or they completely retreat and run away.

Adolescence is, also, a period when there is a deep concern about the future and the kind of work or profession the adolescent will eventually pursue. Many with poor self-images are constantly questioning their ability to achieve in anything, or they overestimate their potentiality, and the real world with its demands shocks them into a sharp reversal. Making a good salary and possessing certain luxuries are often the parent's transferred goals for them. Hopefully, an adolescent's self-assertion in the choice of his own goal and the way to achieve it can offset his depression, severe in some instances unto suicide.

ASSESSMENT

When one initially judges that a particular behavior problem of an adolescent might not only have a total impact on a family unit but might, also, be perceived as the expressed pain of all the members, one should not structure the exploratory process without involving all of the family members. In this way, a more adequate assessment can be determined. This requirement of interviewing the family members together is based on the assumption that the therapist can understand and assess the part that the family interaction plays in producing the problem and its significance in the family's ongoing life only if the therapist can observe family interaction directly.[6] Scheduling for purposes of diagnostic assessment should, then, initially include all the members of the family. Although initial resistance is the name of the game that family members play, many agencies have set as their policy: "If all of the family members are not present, then there is no interview, and no solution to the problem can be arrived at." Exceptions to this policy may be made when severe individual pathology—for example, psychosis—would destroy any attempts at communication. Ackerman reflects:[7]

The therapist's submission to a parent's or family member's refusal to attend a family interview is usually unwise. When one member balks, he is not acting alone. This is usually a symptom of a split family, a war between opposing factions. One must reach out for all sides. Sometimes parents obsessed with one child's (adolescent's) disturbance are resistant to bringing in the whole family. They express fear of contaminating the other children. It is the therapist's responsibility to test the genuineness and validity of such protests. . . . The parents may be hiding behind their children. Often this is a defensive facade concealing a pseudo-secret in the family which the therapist must penetrate.

I, personally, chose to approach the family differentially. While I stress the need to see all the family members together, I find that there are many difficult situations which might make this impossible. My aim, then, is to work toward a total family presence. Furthermore, I do not consider the agency office a consecrated place; home interviews are especially recommended when there are pre-school children or one member is fully or partially disabled.

In the first interview, the therapist makes the family aware that the characteristic or critical modes of family interaction have a critical bearing on the adolescent's problem.[8] Immediately, the adolescent comes to perceive what his particular behavior problem means to his family. Highlighting the fact that the adolescent's pain is the pain of the total family diminishes his culpability and exposes the scapegoating to which this family has resorted in order to maintain its homeostasis, its precarious equilibrium.[9] In the process, distortions, denials, and projections are exposed; family secrets are hinted at; family alliances are manifested; subtle family roles are brought out into the open. The entire communication process is revealed for the first time. Destructive defenses of silence and withdrawal are literally played out. Distorted family rules, together with subtle parental cues, are exposed. Who expresses anger in this family? Who dominates and controls? Who determines what is loyalty and disloyalty in their respective actions?

And as all the buried traumatic past and present come to light, the therapist is able "to assess whether the intrapsychic distortions of the adolescent are firmly fixated and resistant to changes within the environment, or whether such distortions are still in a state of fluidity and primarily reinforced, daily, by parental cueing."[10] What, for instance, are the cues that frankly encourage sexual involvement? What subtle signs are given that allow for stealing, strong aggressive behavior, educational failure? And, above all, how manifest are the double-bind messages that are sent out with regularity and lead to deep confusion, anxiety, and guilt, in fact, at times becoming the base for certain schizophrenic reactions? As Satir sums it up: "Because the conflict within the messages is hidden and the child has been trained not to 'see' it as the source of his disturbance, he turns the blame on himself."[11] But covertly, he uses a disguised protest, one which society calls "crazy" or "sick" behavior.

But above all, this diagnostic phase often reveals the turmoil in the marital relationship itself, which is covered up by the scapegoating of the problem teenager. Many therapists agree that the marital relationship is the axis around which all other relationships are formed, and that a pained marital relationship tends to produce dysfunctional parenting. A scapegoated adolescent is most obviously affected by this, and his symptoms are an "SOS" about his parents' pain and the resulting family imbalance. His symptoms are also a message that he is distorting his own growth as a result of trying to alleviate and absorb his parents' pain.[12] One cannot help notice that when the parental pain is hinted at or even covertly mentioned, there is an immediate resistance to such a revelation by the flow being directed back to the adolescent's symptoms. Many of us have noticed how the adolescent himself will often protect his parents in this and bring attention back to himself. Satir herself is so convinced of the relationship between symptoms and pain that she championed a modality which looked primarily to the pained marital relationship as the causal nexus. Noteworthy, also, is the abatement of adolescent symptoms when the parents realize the true situation and reach out for help for themselves.

Finally, in the diagnostic process, a worker needs to determine the helping workability of the particular family. "To participate in family unit therapy, the family needs to begin with or develop some wish, ability and tolerance for working on the problem."[13] Does this family have the strength to look honestly at the causality of an adolescent's symptoms? Is their homeostasis so rigidified that it could not be altered to allow for a more dynamic fluidity which would allow for differences? Such a determination is all important if one is considering group treatment for the entire family with periods for individual therapy of the adolescent and/or counseling for the marital pair themselves.

THERAPEUTIC INTERVENTION

At this time, when both the maturational tasks of parents and their adolescent children are under fire and often, in open conflict, it is most helpful, when ordinary means are failing, that some form of therapeutic intervention with all of the family members be introduced. Our recommendation is for some form of family treatment. In this type of intervention, the conflict is brought to the fore, to center stage, and all the issues highlighted. The dependency-independency, the questions of role behavior, and modes of communication, the clash of values and standards, the upsurge of sexual identification and sexual struggle, are sorted out in the family forum and studied and regarded in their relation to all of the family members.

First of all, there is a noticeable decrease in adolescent anxiety when the realization of total family involvement diffuses the scapegoating role.[14] Problems of similarities and differences, connectedness and separateness, heighten the juxtaposition of contrasts, but within the therapeutic milieu, their sharp edges begin to lose their power to hurt and anger. Different opinions are being listened to for the first time. The threat of their revelation no longer destroys union. Uniqueness is celebrated and no longer becomes the death knell of family togetherness. And the adolescent is stunned into recognizing that working together is possible, that the love for each other can be rekindled and recaptured, that he has a mother and a father who care for him and recognize their own mistakes. I cannot stress enough what the initial diminution of the adolescent's anxiety does to the adolescent himself. He cannot believe it! Doubt plagues him, but he is beginning to hope, and any individual sessions held with him enable him to look at himself away from the continuous projective method he is wont to adopt to answer all of his problems. He is, also, very curious about the marital sessions set up with his parents, but he is very frankly told to mind his own business, letting his parents handle their own mutual problems, and advised to stop making his way of life a reaction to his parents' struggles.[15]

In contrast to this, by way of a resistive pattern, an adolescent can stir up his parents' anxiety when he struggles with his own feelings of separation. "It's O.K. I won't eat or sleep as well. But I'll be all right in my new pad."

As parents unravel their role differences and seek to uncover the initial love that first attracted them to each other, the adolescent begins to perceive, crudely at first, some manifestation of love for him. Because the parents are rediscovering each other, the symbiosis of a particular parent begins to diminish. Sexual seductiveness, overt or hidden, also decreases, or the game of sexual denial or downgrading is no longer played. Consequently, the true, underlying love begins to manifest itself, and no longer does it appear that working on the conflict will destroy everybody involved. Certainly, the battles continue, but the fact that his parents really care, really recognize him as a person, diminishes the threat that they will abandon him forever. And a *changed* family structure does not mean a *destroyed* family structure. It has now been recast, reshaped for the better, and he now has an important role as a sharing, responsible member.

As the respective parent's battle for the loyalty of the adolescent begins to evanesce, the adolescent begins to discover his own sexual identification. Sexual competitiveness between the parents for the adolescent's identification only destroys or reduces the adolescent to an unsexed pawn. A healthy respect for their child's identification and uniqueness helps the "king" and "queen" to limit the fray to themselves. Regressions and growth, consistent with maturational changes, are defined for each group and are limited to each.[16]

I must note how the therapist often needs to set himself up as a role model in the struggle that emanates around differences in values and standards. There is the constant need to clarify, assess, and determine what set of values is being challenged or reorganized. Values appear on different levels, and often, parents latch on to those which are not that important. The right to work it out for oneself, the right to think it through for oneself, becomes the source of the initial litigation. The historical past in their own lives and its recall often help parents to understand the historical present in the lives of their adolescent children. Both sides test out their ideas with the therapist; both sides use the therapist as the communications middleman and barterer. The discovery of the evolution of change amidst stability heightens the position of relative versus absolute. A climate of trust needs to be developed, and compromise should not be considered a dirty word.

Often, individual therapy with a passive youngster leads to a more assertive, even aggressive behavior pattern. Parents become confused and tend to remove their youngster from such sessions. Parents need careful explanations and guidance to understand these patterns, especially if the adolescent's tendency is to display these new powers by provocative acts.

As the adolescent grows up and plans to leave the family, parents often transfer the role of scapegoating to the next adolescent in line.[17]—thus the need in the planning for the initial family treatment session to have all of the family members involved, not just the particular adolescent and his parents. Conflicts tend to perpetuate themselves unless their sources are realistically handled and eliminated. A younger brother or sister is very much involved in the family interaction. Sometimes, a kind of parental expectancy declares his role in the family hierarchy, and if he wants their "love," he fulfills that role. Being a part of the family treatment, appreciably helps him not to follow previous footsteps and to understand how his parents' separation anxiety has to be handled in a different way.

No matter how much the parents protest, and no matter how much they declare the adolescent to be the main problem, it is essential that the parents be seen by themselves. Startling facets and dynamics almost always appear, and often, parents thank me for pushing them into this dyadic intervention. Often, I have been surprised by the switch in attitude which takes place. A demanding wife suddenly becomes demure and almost seductive. Key problems in their sexual relationship swiftly come to notice and their "pain" with each other catches up with the idealistic promise of the rosy past.[18] Romanticism is often laughed at, and the critical, hurtful communications are at least ventilated, sometimes even with surprise that they could express these before a "stranger."

And I am not adverse to individual therapy with the adolescent; in fact, in my own practice, it generally goes hand in hand with the family treatment.[19] The same problems can appear in both forums. For instance, dependency can cause an adolescent to be an underachiever in his educative or peer performances. Or certain sexual problems need to be discussed. In both instances, I share by role-playing what I shall communicate with his parents until he is satisfied and understands that his confidence will not be used in such a way that might cause him difficulty. Parents often deny their roles as primary instructors of sex because of the possible seductive aspect of the parental relationship and appear happy, almost relieved, when certain "delicate" areas are mentioned as having been discussed with their children.

In summary, my own practice experience has led me to believe that family sessions involving all of the family members are most helpful when intermeshed with individual interviews with the adolescent (and in some instances, group sessions with other peer members)[20] and with separate interviews with the marital couple.[21] But by saying this, I am not negating family unit treatment as the sole interventive approach. Often, the careful differential assessment of the adolescent problem might be the controlling key in having family treatment as the sole therapeutic modality. Consider, for instance, certain kinds of family symbiosis when the adolescent identification is diffused among the family members to such a point that individual identity exists only in family identity. Minuchin provided the classic case in this when he discussed how an adolescent's individuation broke through in the form of an idiosyncratic and life-defying self-starvation, in the symptoms of anorexia nervosa.[22] The family therapists took on a very active role setting up family tasks that highlighted the family's internal power plays and eventually, forcing a disruption of the family's pathologic equilibrium. While there was no passivity in their approach, there was no separate one-to-one relationship with the adolescent to encourage his individuation. As the youngster was already secretly in control of his entire family, with the symptom of anorexia, and as the parents were already helpless, the family therapy merely brought to the surface and underscored that the boy was truly the despot and that the family as a total unit needed to combat this.

John Bell also proposed family treatment as the sole therapeutic modality when individual members were trying to prevent the therapist from dealing with the total family and from achieving the therapeutic goal of balanced opportunities for self-expression.[23] When the situation is truly a family situation and there is great need to reflect on its effect on the whole family, one must resist any insistance to compartmentalize or discuss this situation with an individual member, shifting the basis of the therapy away from the family.

In the case he presented, Dr. Bell very carefully indicated the availability of other therapists for individual consultation but continued to emphasize the necessity for the total family approach. His own personal conviction of the correctness of his assessment helped him to hold the line even though the suasive and colluding forces were very strong. He pointed out that "hidden material" would eventually have to be presented to all family members and advocated that it be shared at that time in the family forum. "You see, I'm here to hear about what goes on in the family and not just to hear about those things which are private to you as individuals—that you can't talk about in front of the other members of the family."[24] "Secrets" can be very hurtful to the entire communication process which needs to be developed, and eventually, with a therapist's patience and openness setting the norm, the secret can be brought forward and discussed. Dr. Bell further advanced that any similar resistive maneuvers such as lingering on to talk with the therapist after the others had left or wanting to discuss issues in private phone calls should also be recognized for what they truly are and blocked from the beginning.[25]

"POSITION Z"

Most early family therapists were originally trained in some form of individual therapy, and their theoretical orientations usually reflect their professional background. Now, with the development of the theoretical formulations of systems and communication, and with the family system being studied through these formulations, many recent students of family therapy are focusing exclusively on a family systems orientation. In 1970, the Committee on the Family Group for the Advancement of Psychiatry discussed three positions in approaches to family treatment.[26] The last group, "Position Z," is of particular interest to us in this part of our paper, and it is a position which I generally favor in working with troubled adolescents. They maintain that many therapists who do not grasp the significance of the family system are not really doing family therapy but treating the adolescent, for instance, in the presence of the family. In fact, Position Z views their approach as a new orientation to psychiatry. They shift the unit of diagnosis and treatment from the single person to the processes between people and define psychopathology as a relationship problem.

Position Z sees the family system as needing some individual to express the pathology of the system, and an intrapsychic process is caused by the relationship situation. Thus, an adolescent can be one contributor to, and an essential part of, a continuing sequence of events among all the people involved and to intervention attempts to change a sequence of behavior involving several of the family.

For example, in an interview a sequence may be identified as follows: the father will be interrogating the child and the child will weakly protest; at a certain point the mother will come to the support of the child and attack the father; the father will then back down and apologize. After a while, the sequence will begin again and repeat itself. The Position Z therapist will see the sequence occur and when it starts again, he will intervene while the father is interrogating the child, just before the mother comes in to attack the father, or just before the father backs down. His goal is to give the sequence a different outcome, and he may or may not point out to the family the nature of the sequence.[27]

The Position Z therapist emphasizes the present situation as the major causal factor and the process that must be changed. He inquires about the past only when he cannot understand the present more easily if it is framed as something from the past. In general, he assumes that a current problem must be currently reinforced if it is continuing to exist.[28]

These therapists tend to work with minimal information. Following some of the basic formulations of crisis intervention theory, they see the first interview as particularly significant and intervene as rapidly as possible. Formal diagnosis, while not abrogated, is perceived more as allaying the therapist's anxiety and thus, they advocate speedy treatment judgments in order to effect speedy change, and they end the first therapy session by helping the family to see that some goal has already been accomplished and that this particular session was actually the therapeutic experience itself. They tend, generally, to brief therapy and maintain that in crisis, a family can move surely and swiftly to attain a great deal. Thus, they propose that "adolescent schizophrenia should be resolved with family treatment at the time of acute onset of the family crisis and not after the adolescent has been hospitalized and the family stabilized."[29] They see change as progressing in discontinuous steps, but a particular change is designated concretely and the family then helped to move swiftly to the next stage in order to prevent slippage.

A Z therapist has little enthusiasm for the idea that interpreting feelings and attitudes brings about change. When dealing, for instance, with hostility between family members, he regards it as a protective act and seeks not to make the hostility explicit but to resolve the difficulties which are causing the hostility in the relationship.

A Position Z therapist sees himself as caught up in the maelstrom of the family. He becomes involved in the struggle of family factions. "These family members are showing *me* how hostile they are to each other." Thus, he includes himself in the very context of the treatment and carefully reviews how he himself might be causing a particular family problem and how he might work in such a way within the family so as to bring about change.

He puts special stress on the communication of all and shows himself uncomfortable if certain members are not talking. Also, he explicitly suggests that they talk to each other, not just to him. He is involved, also, in the total ecological system and maintains that he must deal, too, with the wider treatment context.

This allows for more opportunities to experiment when a particular approach is not working. He may attempt multiple-family therapy and network therapy in which not only the family but friends and neighbors are brought into the treatment sessions. In short, though Z therapists tend to feel that any firmly delineated set of procedures is a handicap, and though they try differentially to fit the modality to the particular family, using at times other units—a single person, a marital pair, etc.—they are generally engaged in family unit treatment, seeing a family regularly or irregularly for several hours at certain times in the conviction that this will save months of regularly spaced sessions.

Finally, Position Z family therapists argue that therapists must share with behavioral scientists that psychiatric problems are steeped in the social milieu which is made up of the interlocking systems of the social institutions. Therapy must, then, look to developing a new ecological framework which does not tend to fragment either conceptually or in treatment but presents a bold backdrop for change within the family.

COUNTER-INDICATIONS IN THE USE OF FAMILY THERAPY

I feel that it would be most helpful to practitioners to discuss in the final section of this paper some counter-indications for the use of family treatment in attempting to help a particular adolescent.

Although there are some family therapists who believe that the question of indications and contraindications is a "non-question," there are many who have written about this subject.[30]

Jackson (1959)[31] distinguished among four categories of

families. In his third category, "unstable, unsatisfactory," a family is experiencing severe psychopathology, and the patient's minimal recovery often poses a serious threat to the parents. There is only limited success in treating these families. In his fourth category, "stable, unsatisfactory," Jackson describes a reaction to a critical comment made against a mother by an older son: immediately, chaos ensued. The mother and father were both hospitalized with serious medical problems, and the older son himself was involved in a car accident. Because money was needed for medical bills, the adolescent patient was sent to a state hospital.

Wynne (1965)[32] lists some severe depressions, some severe masochistic states, and acute schizophrenia as strong counterindicators. Implied contraindications relate to situations in which a stable, structured treatment set-up is not possible and when a skilled family therapist is not available.

Ackerman (1966)[33] lists some eight contraindications:

(1) When there is a process of a malignant, irreversible trend toward breakup of the family, which may mean that it is too late to reverse the process of fragmentation;

(2) When there is the dominance within the group of a concentrated focus of malignant, destructive motivation;

(3) When there is one parent who is afflicted with an organized progressive paranoid condition, or with incorrigible psychopathic destructiveness, or who is a confirmed criminal or pervert;

(4) Parents, one or both, who are unable to be sufficiently honest; lying and deceitfulness that are deeply rooted in the group negate the potential usefulness of family therapy;

(5) The existence of a certain kind of valid family secret;

(6) The existence of an unyielding cultural, religious, or economic prejudice against this form of intervention;

(7) The existence in some members of extremely rigid defenses which, if broken, might induce a psychosis, a psychosomatic crisis, or physical assault;

(8) Finally, the presence of organic disease or other disability of a progressive nature that precludes the participation of one or more members.

Kramer (1970)[34] discusses a firm decision to divorce, severe psychotic depression, and hard core psychopathy as strong contraindicators. He also mentions the period when a therapist is converting from individual to family therapy.

Howells (1972) has found family therapy unsuccessful in families with a member who suffers from "process schizophrenia," a diagnostic entity more clearly defined in Europe than in the United States. Many would probably disagree with this.

Whitaker (1968)[35] deplores the use of an unskilled family therapist and even insists on the use of two therapists who respect each other and even rescue one another from overinvolvement.

Haley (1971),[36] understood in his own frame of reference, discusses the disquieting effects on a clinic of the introduction of family therapy methods in which there is the abandonment of highly cherished theoretical systems to that of interpersonal theories and the adoption of an action-oriented point of view. He also mentions the disturbances that will take place within the standard out-patient clinic when new family therapists, coming in as lower paid professionals, are upsetting the staid approaches of the less-skilled but higher-paid professionals.

CONCLUSION

In conclusion, it might be said that family therapy does offer a way of more adequately overcoming an adolescent's problems and his own resistance to change. Used in many treatment situations, it can serve to offer a different approach, a different *modus operandi*, not just for the sake of change but because it embodies a respect for an adolescent's individuation as well as respect for the family group and its own identity. It definitely affects better communication and feelings of intimacy without allowing for a drift back toward the infantile and the erotic. It can be used alone or together with other kinds of therapy with a guard on the necessary precautions.

An adolescent's "changing seasons" can be fraught with a hectic upheaval and deep confusion. Stability within one's self as a therapist, using family treatment as a helping guide, seeks to stabilize the shifting, overwhelming, and conflictual forces that run riot in the adolescent's life and in the life of his family.

FOOTNOTES

1. Ivan Boszormenyi-Nagy and James Framo (eds.), *Intensive Family Therapy* (New York, 1969), p. XVII.
2. Rae B. Weiner, "Adolescent Problems: Symptoms of Family Dysfunction," *Social Casework*, Vol. 47, No. 6. (June, 1966), p. 373.

3. *Ibid.*, p. 373.

4. Nathan Ackerman, *The Psychodynamics of Family Life* (New York, 1958), p. 207.

5. Helm Stierlin, M.D., *Separating Parents and Adolescents* (New York, 1974).

6. Frances Scherz, "Use of Family Interviews in Diagnosis," *Social Casework* (April, 1964), p. 210.

7. N. Ackerman, *Family Therapy in Transition* (New York, 1970), p. 7.

8. Scherz, *op. cit.*, p. 213.

9. Ackerman, *op. cit.*, p. 9.

10. Frank S. Williams, M.D., "Family Therapy: Its Role in Adolescent Psychiatry," in Max Sugar, M.D. (ed.), *The Adolescent in Group and Family Therapy* (New York, 1975), p. 184.

11. Virginia Satir, *Conjoint Family Therapy* (Palo Alto, California, 1967), p. 37.

12. *Ibid.*, pp. 1-2.

13. Frances H. Scherz, "Theories and Practice of Family Therapy," in Robert Roberts and Robert Nee (eds.), *Theories of Social Casework* (Chicago, Illinois, 1970), p. 251.

14. Celia Mitchell, "Casework Approach to Distrubed Families," in Ackerman, Beatman & Sherman (eds.), *Exploring the Base for Family Therapy* (New York, 1961), p. 80.

15. S. Minuchin, *Families and Family Therapy* (Cambridge, Mass., 1974), p. 57.

16. Satir, *op. cit.*, pp. 58-59, 49-53.

17. *Ibid.*, p. 35.

18. Salvador Minuchin, *op. cit.*, pp. 181 ff.

19. *Ibid.* pp. 106, 147.

20. Nathan Ackerman, *The Psychodynamics of Family Life*, pp. 291 ff.

21. Satir, *op. cit.*, p. 167.

22. S. Minuchin, "Reconceptualization of Adolescent Dynamics from the Family Point of View," in D. Offer and J.F. Masterson (eds.), *Teaching and Learning Adolescent Psychiatry* (Springfield, Illinois, 1971). Also see S. Minuchin, *Families and Family Therapy, op. cit.*, pp. 103-104.

23. John E. Bell, *Family Therapy* (New York-London, 1975), pp. 19, 52.

24. *Ibid.*, p. 55

25. *Ibid.*, pp. 57-58.

26. The Committee on the Family Group for the Advancement of Psychiatry, *Treatment of Families in Conflict* (New York, 1970), pp. 47 ff.

27. *Ibid.*, p. 52.

28. *Ibid.*, p. 53.

29. *Ibid.*, p. 54.

30. Daniel Offer and Evert Vander Stoep, "Indications and Contraindications for Family Therapy," in Max Sugar (ed.), *The Adolescent in Group and Family Therapy* (New York, 1975), pp. 145-160.

31. Don Jackson, "Family Interaction, Family Homeostasis and Implication for Therapy," in J. Masserman (ed.), *Individual and Family Dynamics* (New York).

32. L. C. Wynne, "Some Indications and Contraindications for Exploratory Family Therapy," in I. Boszormenyi-Nagy and J. L. Framo (eds.), *Intensive Family Therapy: Theoretical and Practical Aspects* (New York), pp. 289-322.

33. N. W. Ackerman, *Treating the Troubled Family* (New York, 1966), pp. 7-8.

34. C. H. Kramer, "Psychoanalytically Oriented Family Therapy: Ten Year Evolution in a Private Child Psychiatry Practice," (Chicago, Ill., 1970), No. 1., pp. 1-42.

35. J. Haley and L. Hoffman, "An Interview with Carl Whitaker," in *Techniques of Family Therapy* (New York, 1967), pp. 473-480.

36. J. Haley, "Why a Mental Health Clinic Should Avoid Family Therapy," manuscript (Philadelphia, 1971).

THE FAMILY GROUP APPROACH WITH FAMILIES OF CHILDREN IN PLACEMENT

Mary Ann Quaranta

INTRODUCTION

Not too many years ago, it would have been ludicrous to pose the simple question of what is a family. The person who raised any doubts about how a mother, a father, or a child should behave would have been characterized as a fool. But today, we know these are pressing concerns among family sociologists, anthropologists, and those in the helping professions who are seeking to guide troubled families.

Is it that family life-styles have changed that radically, or is it that we are growing more aware of the complexities of family life? Certainly, there have been changes in regard to family structure and in regard to the way in which families function. It is also true that we are learning more and more about family life, which is far more visible than it was in the past. It was more than technology that permitted us to see the Louds on television. Greater openness and more willingness to share family intimacies are part of this changing scene. Also, the tools of social science research are being brought to bear on this most fundamental and yet least studied of our institutions, the family. Jules Henry's *Pathways to Insanity*[1] is another recent example of this greater visibility, and openness, and the greater push toward research on the family.

Group marriage, communal families, and adoption of children by single persons are just a few of the variations in family life-styles that we are observing today. Traditional family forms are obviously on trial. A rapidly growing divorce rate, more trial marriages, women's liberation, legalized abortion, and greater sexual freedom are forcing us to look more closely and more carefully at the family as a social institution.

It might be well to consider how one defines a family. John Bell[2] discusses three definitions of a family. One definition views the family through the eyes of a child who perceives the family as either a benign or a malicious source of happiness or pain. In the traditional model of social work practice, there has been a tendency to use this definition, seeing the family as the main source of an individual's pathology or health. The second definition to which Bell refers, and the one which is gaining value as we begin to reexamine our approach to the family, is the sociological one with emphasis on communication patterns, group attitudes, and family group decisions. In this definition, there is a de-emphasis on the individual and the past with greater focus on the present interactional and transactional aspects of family life. It is this framework which has been particularly useful in the family treatment modality, and it is one which deserves greater study and consideration.

The third definition studies the family as an institution with a focus on values, on allocation of roles and tasks, and on similar issues. It is within this perspective of the family that family lifestyles might be studied, that marriage patterns and the consequences of divorce could be viewed and that the impact of changing sex roles might also be examined.

These developments have coincided with parallel growth in the area of viewing the family as the unit for helping troubled family groups. The major concern of this paper is to consider the particular needs of those families who require care for their children outside of the home. The merits of using the family group treatment model in helping the families is another issue addressed in this paper.

SOME ASSUMPTIONS REEXAMINED

Although there has been a close link between the social work profession and the general societal concern with better family life, social workers have been prone to accept as given some of the common assumptions regarding family life and have not really used their rich experience with families to forge new conceptual or practice frontiers in working with the family. Social work's concern with families has often been in regard to the welfare of children. It is in this context that we have perpetuated a number of assumptions that require and perhaps, demand scrutiny in our work as new knowledge and understanding develop about the family.

One of these assumptions is that there is one model of socialization which insures maximizing a child's potential. The nuclear family unit with a father, a mother, and two children, one of each sex, constitutes that model American family which generations of Americans have considered the ideal. The implicit understanding is that this type of family structure represents the most effective system for socializing children. Considerable reinforcement of this concept has been provided by the Freudian and neo-Freudian personality theories which postulated that successful maturity required a "working-through" of the Oedipal conflict in the nuclear family romance. Based on the validity of this assumption regarding the most desirable type of family care for children, the child welfare field has attempted in a variety of ways to stimulate this model nuclear family for youngsters needing care outside of their own homes.

It is not the purpose of this paper to address the sociological developments and the research evidence that have served to challenge the merits of assuming that the traditional nuclear family is the "best" form of child care. It is necessary to indicate that there are findings to suggest that other types of family structure warrant consideration for their effectiveness in rearing children. The relevance of this issue for child welfare, with its responsibility for caring for the neglected and dependent children of this society, creates the need for the professionals to experiment with different models of substitute family care.

Over this decade, the programatic pendulum of child welfare has shifted from one substitute care approach to another without the benefit of the evaluative research to test the values of such programs. There is now a trend toward group homes which are regarded as a panacea as was boarding care with foster families a few decades ago. It seems apparent that no form of substitute care responds to the needs of all children. What is needed are guidelines on which of the various types of care are best suited to the individual needs of the children.

Another assumption which requires review is that as other institutions such as the school and the welfare systems assume responsibility for certain functions traditionally performed by the family, there occurs an erosion of the family's importance in our society. Perhaps this phenomenon is to be encouraged as it allows the family to become more specialized in some of its functions, paralleling what has occurred in other social institutions. One of the very reasons that the model of the nuclear family is suspect is that of the undue strain placed on its adult members. Our society expects a great deal from the husband/wife-mother/father of the nuclear family. They are to be quite self-sufficient in meeting the needs of their own system, the physical, economic, emotional, and spiritual needs. Their esteem as a unit tends to be threatened if they need to seek help outside of the nuclear unit, even to reaching to other members of the extended family.

Many families are unable to meet these expectations and become the casualties of the system. One of the responsibilities they are often unable to meet is providing adequate care for their young. These are the families whose children require care outside of their own homes. These families are viewed as failures, having been unable to meet society's expectations of a "good" family.

The relevance of these many concerns to child welfare seems poignant when we realize that too often, children have been removed and separated from their own homes and later, from foster homes for reasons related to these assumptions and values regarding preferred family models and life-styles. How many children have been separated from their natural families because those families did not measure up to the expectations we have of families in our society? It seems particularly essential to examine some of these assumptions in relation to our work with minority children and their families. It is with these families that we must raise our consciousness of, and sensitivity to, life-style variations which often are, or seem to be, at variance with the middle class expectations about family life and the ways in which it meets the needs of children. Yet we know precious little about the effectiveness of these variations in meeting the basic needs of children.

It is incumbent upon us to consider these and other issues as we design and implement costly child welfare programs, often without the kind of evidence which would be required in a comparably large industrial organization. Our assumptions, values, concepts, practices, and programs need to be put on trial for their relevance to the needs of the children, those in their own homes and those under care outside their homes.

MORE WORK WITH NATURAL FAMILIES

One of the concerns in child welfare today is the need to provide greater involvement of the natural families. There is a growing consciousness among social workers that in the profession's child centeredness, it has tended to overlook the natural families of children under care. Although child care agencies claim that the natural parent is a client who will be helped and rehabilitated for later reunion with the child, there is reason to question what measure of resources has been allocated to this objective and what order or priority this item has on agency agendas.

In general, the biological families of the placed child constitute the downtrodden of our society, the disinherited, the so-called hard core, the disadvantaged families.[3] There are certain characteristics which we can vividly associate with the natural families: they are usually beset by a host of concrete problems in regard to their poor economic conditions, particularly seen in problems with employment, housing, and health; alcoholism, illegitimacy, delinquency, criminality, divorce, suicide, child neglect, and child-abuse are just some of the common problems which affect these families. They are families who are particularly unable to perform the basic functions of a family, especially the primary ones which are to socialize the young and to meet the affective needs of the members. Child-rearing is problematic often because of a structural problem or a missing parent, usually the father. Too, parents in these high risk families are often inconsistent and irresponsible, at times authoritarian and controlling and at other times, they ignore the child's need for adult guidance. A parent may assume a child's role, and a child may be called upon to assume parenting functions: children may have to separate fighting parents. Psychological problems abound in these families, and it is frequently difficult to tell which come first, the overwhelming social problems or the personality problems.

There is a growing literature around child advocacy on behalf of the legal, civil, and social rights of the child. Perhaps, some of the methodical and programming expertise which is being developed regarding child advocacy will be used in a parallel movement which champions the rights of the natural family. Perhaps it is timely to begin to channel some of the fiscal support being used to maintain children *outside* their homes to support these same children *in* their homes. More than seven million of the seventy-six million children in this country live in fatherless homes, yet what services have been provided to help these families? Let us imagine allocating some of the money it costs to provide foster care for a child to the child's family in order to help to solve its economic, housing, and health problems. The family could then purchase necessary supporting services such as homemaking, counseling, and the like. Unquestionably, supporting services might prevent many of these children from entering foster care programs.

There has been a tendency for child welfare agencies to discount the resources of natural families and to take a somewhat biased view of their role in relation to the child. Maximum feasible participation of natural parents in decision making and planning for their children should be a guiding principle. For instance, we must ask ourselves why we do not invite the parents of placed children to participate in conferences when planning for their children occurs.

Once we accept the premise that the child welfare field needs to address itself more fully in its program and in its professional processes to the needs of natural families, the implications for budgetary allocations, programming, and the deployment of staff would have to be considered.

THE FAMILY GROUP APPROACH WITH NATURAL FAMILIES

A major theme of this paper is to suggest that a modality which seems to suggest possibilities for more effective work with natural families is the use of a family group approach. Before considering some specific implications for child welfare practice, it might be well to consider some of the main tenets of this approach: family treatment is a method of intervention which engages an entire family group in pursuing and negotiating feasible solutions to its current problems as a family. It defines the present as reflecting the past and anticipating the future. Priority is placed on possible change and growth through problem-solving rather than on isolating causes and eliminating symptoms. The focus of intervention is the interactional and transactional patterns in the family as it functions as a social system.

There has been a number of theoretical developments which have assisted in advancing the understanding of family dynamics:

new knowledge of the adaptive functions of the ego, small group theory, communication theory, and particularly, systems theory have promoted a deeper understanding of family relationships and the relationship between families and other segments of society. This new understanding has enabled us to view the family not as a collection of individuals but as a social system transacting with other social systems in the community where the family is situated. Emphasis is placed on the distribution of power and on communication patterns idiosyncratic to particular families.

It might be well to consider a few guidelines which may apply in engaging natural families in this interventive modality. Obviously, the first step in implementing the family approach is the decision to meet with the entire family as the unit of professional attention. Who should make this decision? A social worker? The natural family? The foster family? Or the child? It seems to this writer that the child should have a large role in making this decision as to how he defines his family. The age of the child would, naturally, be a factor in influencing the extent of the child's role, remembering, of course, that young children have ideas and feelings which must be given enormous weight.

In regard to work with the natural family as the unit of attention, too often, social workers have used the nuclear family structure as the norm, dismissing other family structures as deviant and "untreatable" when what is needed is more flexibility and openness in defining the family's structure and its functions. Often, the natural families are one-parented with another adult serving paternal functions. We have to think of the role of significant others who may not actually be living with the family but who may have great influence in their lives.

Important to consider, too, is programming sessions when the child in care can be present. The placed child is often the scapegoat caught in the maze of the natural family's problems and projections and carrying the family's pathology and guilt, to say nothing of the conflict of the child being caught in between the natural family and the surrogate family and all that this implies. It is essential that sessions with the biological family, the foster family, or the cottage parents be held with the child present.

The emphasis on the here and now in family group approaches is appropriate for work with the biological families who are oppressed with current problems, many of them very concrete. The family worker will have to demonstrate awareness of the burden of these problems if the essential climate of trust is to be developed.

Disadvantaged families often have particular problems in communication, relying usually on non-verbal communication for conveying feelings to one another. Such a non-verbal system is the one to which the placed children are socialized. The family social worker can play an important role in helping the family members to put their thoughts and feelings into words for one another. The worker can play the role of mediator and broker, helping the family members not only to share their feelings but also, to verbalize and label them in a way which promotes more open communication.[4]

Family sessions require an active, energetic worker who can maintain focus and who can keep the interactional volley alive with good therapeutic purpose. The family worker uses a wide repertoire of techniques including raising questions, making interpretations, giving advice, setting rules, demonstrating behavior, role playing, and confrontation. Central to all of this is the need for a strong, aggressive leadership of the session. Wishy-washy, lukewarm neutrality and passivity are not games you can play in family work. Above all, you must take pleasure in the experience, for if you do not, it is very evident to the family. You need confidence in yourself and in the value and effectiveness of your work. You need to be open, unafraid to make mistakes, and able to experiment with each family and in each interview. This open and confident posture is particularly important in working with the disadvantaged families of placed children, families which are looking to the social worker's legitimate professional authority for information and guidance.

The modality of working with the family as a group appears to lend itself to prevention of placement and to the needs of the families of children whose placement was not provided. From the very point of planning placement, this approach would prove useful in helping to reduce the double-binds, the scapegoating, and the distortion in communication that occur with so many persons (members of natural and foster families and the social worker) to whom the child and the family must relate. Such family sessions would also aid in working through the child's conflicts while in placement as well as the family role in considering "permanent" planning for the child.

SUMMARY

There is a rapidly growing interest in an awareness of the family not only as an institution which is undergoing dramatic changes but also in regard to the issues of structure and function in family life. This phenomenon is paralleled by an increasing use of the family group as the unit of therapeutic attention.

There is no area where this knowledge and expertise is as needed as in work with those children who must be cared for outside of their own homes. Some of the assumptions surrounding family life which have been the bases for child welfare programs must be scrutinized for their current validity. With the understanding that no one model of surrogate family care would meet the needs of all children, we need greater clarity regarding which types of children are best served by the alternative models of substitute care.

The developments in family group approaches appear to have merit in work with troubled families who are beset with social and psychological problems. Preventive work with these families might help them to keep their children in their homes. The family group approach can, also, be utilized with biological families after the children are placed either to facilitate the child's early return to the home or to establish a permanent plan for the child.

FOOTNOTES

1. Jules Henry, *Pathways to Insanity* (New York, 1965).
2. John E. Bell, "Recent Advances in Family Group Therapy." *Theory and Practice of Family Psychiatry* (New York, 1971).
3. A recent study which provides an excellent picture of the families of 624 children under care in New York City is that by Shirley Jenkins and Elaine Norman, *Filial Deprivation and Foster Care* (New York, 1972).
4. Salvador Minuchin's *Families of the Slums* (New York, 1967) is a useful reference for further elaboration in work with disadvantaged families.

PART FOUR

SPECIFIC TECHNIQUES
AND ISSUES

INTRODUCTION

While discussing the reasons he became a family therapist, Augustus Napier wrote in 1971, "I hate the establishment, and orthodoxy, and family therapy is now a convenient rebellion."[1] That statement serves to remind us that as little as five years ago, family therapy was still considered an unorthodox and rebellious form of treatment. Few, today, would categorize it that way. Scholarly books and articles pour out on the subject; training institutes have sprung up throughout the country, university graduate programs focusing on the area are appearing, practitioners have begun to proliferate. Family therapy has left its unorthodox image behind and has entered the therapeutic establishment.

The method itself is no longer a "convenient rebellion." The trappings of maturity have been achieved. No one would dispute, however, that further growth is needed. Such growth should include further explication of theory, further exploration of useful techniques within the family treatment modality, and further attention and responsiveness to changing life-styles, attitudes, and values influencing the modern family.

This last part of the present monograph deals with the latter two considerations. The first paper addresses the pros and cons of the introduction of a co-therapist into the therapeutic situation. The second paper concerns itself with the issue of changing attitudes toward gender or sex, role allocations in our society today, and the import of such changes for family therapists.

FOOTNOTES

1. Andrew Ferber, Marilyn Mendelsohn, and Augustus Napier, (eds.), *The Book of Family Therapy* (Boston, Mass., 1973), p. 96.

USE OF CO-THERAPISTS IN FAMILY TREATMENT

Victoria Olds

THE FAMILY SYSTEM AS FOCUS OF TREATMENT

Luthman and Kirschenbaum stress the interactional framework as basic to the family group. They define "system as the complex of patterns of behavior and ways of functioning with one another which family members believe necessary in order for family to survive and perform its tasks."[1] According to Minuchin, individuals in a family are members of the social system, acting and re-acting within that system. Any changes within the system contribute to changes in the behavior and in the inner psychic processes of all the members of that system.[2]

The therapists become an integral part of the family system when treatment tasks are undertaken. Consequently, the behavior of the therapists is significant to the entire process within the system.

The presence of an identified patient is symptomatic evidence of some malfunctions within the family system. The interlocking family pathology is frequently expressed by the deviant or problematic behavior of one of the family members. The intervention of the therapists serves to modify the interactions within the family system and to direct the strengths in the family toward healthy growth.

Carl Whitaker has said that a healthy family is one which can achieve for its members a high level of togetherness and a high degree of individuation. The keynotes are flexibility and responsiveness in relationships. Family members are free to form meaningful relationships outside the home as well as to change roles in their intrafamily relationships in response to changing situations.

Also, the healthy family unit makes connections with extended family ties and friendship networks in its environment.

The family system encompasses a number of sub-systems: dyads such as the parents, a parent-child, a child-child, or a triangle whereby a parent-child join to isolate the other parent, or two children maneuver to scapegoat a third sibling. The assigned roles of family members in the system resist change. In a disturbed family system, the scapegoated member, identified as the patient, may be the glue which holds the family together. Thus, the family may resist efforts to have the system changed and may muster much energy to defeat the work of the therapists.

However, at times of stress and crisis, the equilibrium or homeostasis of the family system becomes shaky. New groupings of members, reassignment of roles, and more adaptive patterns become possible. When a family member enters or leaves the family, or when environmental or structural changes take place, conditions in the home become more amenable to change. At these times, the work of the therapists is strategic.

CO-THERAPY AS A METHOD OF CHOICE

Just as there is no general agreement as to a standard procedure in family therapy, there is no consensus as to the superiority of co-therapy as a method of intervention. According to the 1970 G.A.P. Report, there are many variations of working with families.[3] Family therapy as a treatment modality can mean treatment of the nuclear family, or the extended family, or just the marital dyad. It can consist of conjoint therapy a la Satir,[4] multiple family therapy,[5] or network therapy.[6]

The work of the family therapist is highly individual and reflects the style of the therapist. Some are dynamically active, provocative, and openly directive such as Ackerman, Minuchin, and Satir. Others, also effective therapists, are less directive and follow the lead of the family like Lyman Wynne, Carl Whitaker, Jay Haley, and Gerald Zuk.

Some therapists like Carl Whitaker see co-therapy as the preferred method of working with families. Whitaker maintains that for him, the co-therapist is an essential support.[7]

On the other hand, Clifford Sager does not approve of co-therapy because he feels one therapist is adequate to the task. Other therapists are on the fence. Yalom[8] states that co-therapy "may have some special advantages but many potential hazards as well." Friedman[9] feels his work was more effective with a co-therapist. Luthman and Kirschenbaum[10] have been committed to co-therapy for over ten years and incorporated this approach into their training programs in California. Kuehn[11] questions the value of co-therapy.

Another development is to have husband-wife teams as co-therapists as the working out of the co-therapy relationship has many similarities to the continuing working out of a marriage relationship. At the Family Institute of Chicago, Dr. Charles Kramer and Mrs. Jeannette Kramer give workshops on how one's own family experiences influence the therapist's treatment style and vice versa. At the Boston Family Institute, another married couple, Fred and Bunny Duhl, give similar seminars.

Co-therapy is more complex, more time-consuming, more expensive, and more difficult to arrange. Why bother then? In this writer's opinion, the advantages benefit the family and also, the therapists. The dynamics of a family interview are so multi-faceted that an individual therapist is under stress to be every-where all at once: to be alert to the words spoken as well as to the feelings underneath, to tune in on the responses of all members of the family simultaneously, and to be interacting verbally and emotionally while making mental observations for future refer-ence. The therapist's task is great if there is only one patient. It becomes enormous with a family as patient. There are so many demands, and the emotional commitment is very heavy.

With co-therapists, the tasks can be shared. One therapist can observe while the other makes comments. The presence of two therapists re-creates the authority of a two-parent family. Indi-vidual family members can reach out to either therapist as needed, and neither the family nor the therapists need feel "trapped" in a complicated relationship.

The co-therapists can serve as role models for the family in expressing agreement or disagreement without being destruc-tive. They can be alert to efforts of the family to split up the therapists into "good" and "bad" parents. The combined efforts of both therapists may become necessary to exert enough lever-age to persuade the family to change.

The co-therapists can offer each other emotional support, share their feelings of frustration, doubt, or satisfaction as the treatment situation develops. In addition, the therapists can en-joy working together. If they can share their own good humor and affection for one another during the family session, the benefits will accrue to the family, and the family will respond and grow.

THE CO-THERAPIST AS A FAMILY MEMBER

In family therapy, the co-therapists keep in mind that they are functioning in families on several levels: they carry roles from their own families of origin in which they had parents, grandparents, and perhaps, siblings. They have roles in a conjugal family or similar relationships. They may be parents. They become involved in the treatment family's problems and relationships. They are in a dyadic relationship with each other before, during, and after the family therapy session. If there is a consultant or a seminar of observers, there are further expectations of analyzing one's roles. The therapists are aware that the power of the family in nurturing its members is such that an individual can derive the greatest emotional gratifications but also, deep personal hurt from family interactions. Roles assigned in childhood can persist throughout life and are worked over continuously by being re-created in new situations.

The demands on the therapist are to develop self-understanding and to become aware of the role identifications, the family secrets, myths, rules, priorities, values, in-jokes, prejudices, etc.. This process is shared regularly with the co-therapist, usually during pre-session conference before the family interview and afterward at post-sessions. The value of openness between the therapists is crucial. The two therapists thus develop greater understanding of each other and can deepen their abilities to work together as a therapeutic team.

SOME STEPS IN CO-THERAPY PROCEDURES

Prior to the first contact with the family, the co-therapists will discuss at a pre-session several areas: their own feelings at that time toward themselves and any stresses or pressures that may interfere with their work, their feelings about each other, in order to clear away any doubts or irritations which may have been lingering. Some of the objectives in the pre-session are to set the stage for the co-therapists to work together and to prepare each other as much as possible for developments during the sessions. Because co-therapy is a useful method for training therapists, the family interviews are often held behind a one-way mirror with the knowledge and consent of the family. The observers are included in the pre-session and post-session as part of their training experience. One of the co-therapists can be a beginning therapist and can learn by working with a more experienced therapist.

During a beginning session, in order to learn what the family sees as the problems, the therapists take responsibility for checking with each family member, including children, as to the definition of the problem. Why did each family member come? What does each see that needs to be changed in the family? A therapeutic contract is arrived at, if possible. The rules are set by the therapists as to who in the family is to be involved and when. It is possible to schedule subgroups and to invite in members of the extended family as the situation develops in later sessions.

The therapists "hang loose," are involved, but not "sucked into" the family system. The focus is on what transpires during the family session and how this reflects patterns established within the family system. The therapists are in control, do not take sides, avoid the "blame game" or the family's efforts to label a villain. The need for change in the family does not require that someone carry the blame. Past mistakes and grievances are underplayed. The focus is on what can be done in the present to bring about a better situation. Often, the children in the family are more free to point out viable alternatives for change. Emphasis can be placed on the healthy parts of the family system and on positive relationships.

During the post-session, it is feasible to invite the family to remain and listen to the recapitulation of the co-therapists' reactions and to the comments of the seminar participants if they are present. The family is asked to listen, then react later. It has been my experience that this additional input from the therapists allows the family to view itself from another perspective and to move an extra step in self-awareness and in motivation for change. The family derives another benefit in an increased sense of self-worth when they see how important their situation is to the co-therapists and to the others in the observation room. They have an opportunity to see the co-therapists as role models in conflict resolution and in sharing of ideas and feelings.

SOME COUNTER-INDICATIONS FOR CO-THERAPY

Co-therapy is not feasible where there are too few therapists. There is also a problem when two therapists do not like each other and co-therapy would not be a gratifying experience for them. If at any point, the relationship between the therapists reaches an impasse that cannot be resolved, it is wiser to discontinue the co-therapy or to make a change; otherwise, the family will be placed in a non-therapeutic or dubious situation. If both therapists are unable to attend each session, there should be discussion as to whether the session should take place with only one therapist or be postponed. In conclusion, family therapists who can arrange to practice as co-therapists, have in store an exciting, rewarding, and complex experience.

FOOTNOTES

1. Shirley G. Luthman and Martin Kirschenbaum, *The Dynamic Family* (Palo Alto, California, 1974), p. 13.
2. Salvador Minuchin, *Families and Family Therapy* (Cambridge, Mass., 1974), pp. 9-10.
3. G.A.P. Report y78, Vol. 7 (1970), pp. 525-644.
4. Virginia Satir, *Conjoint Family Therapy* (Palo Alto, California, 1964), pp. 1-8.
5. Peter N. Laqueur, "Mechanisms of Change in Multiple Family Therapy in C.J. Sager and H.S. Kaplan (eds.), *Progress in Group and Family Therapy* (New York, 1972), p. 404.
6. Ross Speck and C.L. Attreave, "Social Network Intervention" in Jay Haley (ed.), *Changing Families* (New York, 1971), p. 312.
7. Carl Whitaker, *Acting Out: Theoretical and Clinical Aspects* (New York, 1965).
8. Irvin D. Yalom, *The Theory and Practice of Group Psychotherapy* (New York, 1970), p. 318.
9. Alfred S. Friedman, "Co-therapy as Family Therapy Method and as a Training Method" in Alfred Friedman (ed.), *Therapy with Families of Sexually Acting-Out Girls* (New York, 1971), p. 36.
10. Luthman, *op. cit.*, p. 193.
11. J. Kuehn, "Sensitivity Training: Interpersonal Overkill and Other Problems," *American Journal of Psychiatry*, Vol. 126 (December, 1969), p. 841.

THE IMPACT OF CHANGING SEX ROLES AND FAMILY THERAPY

Elaine Norman, Ph.D.

In a great number of cases, the underlying pathology of troubled families stems at least in part from the restrictive, frustrating sex role ideology which our society has advocated. Even in family groups where crippling pathology has not yet surfaced, adherence to gender role stereotypes inhibits family growth and intimacy. This paper will speak to that theme and will suggest that family therapists need to approach this area with an open-minded and innovative posture rather than with the restrictive traditional ideology that the mental health professions have been following for so long. (The reader might be interested to know that the writer of this paper is not a family therapist but is a sociologist and a committed feminist with a great personal interest in family therapy.)

We all have in our minds stereotypes which reflect our ideas of masculinity and femininity. Men are expected to be virile, athletic, strong, brave, aggressive, unemotional, rational, dominating, success-oriented, ambitious, confident, decisive. Women are expected to be domestic, maternal, nurturing, passive, emotional, compassionate, intuitive, sensitive, dependent, submissive, shy, affectionate, innocent.[1]

In reality, none of these gender-linked images are inately given, neither inherited, instinctual, nor hormonally sex-linked. Rather, they are culturally derived and differ in different societies and at different historical periods. In some societies, for example, the men are fully as nurturing as, or more so than, the women. In others, it is the women who are expected to be aggressive and the men cooperative and maternal.[2] In still others, it is the men who are expected to be emotional and intuitive while the women are expected to be rational and intellectual. In reality, both sexes have the potential to display all traits. Cultural conditioning and the stereotypes from which such conditioning is derived function as a straightjacket, inhibiting individuals in many ways.

To illustrate, much recent research has indicated that high femininity in women, that is strong acceptance of traditional feminine characteristics, has consistently been related to high anxiety, low self-esteem, and low social acceptance. High masculinity in men has consistently been related to good psychological adjustment *only in adolescence*. During adulthood, it results in high anxiety, high neuroticism and low self-acceptance. In addition, greater intellectual development has been repeatedly related to cross-sex typing, that is, to masculinity in girls and to femininity in boys. Boys and girls who adhere strongly to traditional sex typing have been found to have lower overall intelligence, lower spatial ability, and lower creativity than those who do not.[3]

Gender typing in the United States today extends beyond definitions of masculinity and femininity. It includes two other very important elements: the ideas that the two sexes have different statuses and that the two sexes should do different work.

The first idea basically assumes that men are superior to women and should be dominant over them, especially in their roles of husband and wife. This idea is deeply ingrained in our culture and is supported by many aspects of our social structure. There are many illustrations.

Taking her husband's name and giving up her own at marriage has great emotional significance for a woman. For by this gesture, she symbolically agrees that her status and social class shall from then on, follow her husband's regardless of her own future or present achievements.

In addition, our basic spouse selection and marital development processes encourage male dominance. American men marry women who are shorter, younger, less well educated, and if working, of lower status and lower salary than themselves. When the twenty-three-year-old man marries the twenty-and-a-half-year-old woman, he is likely to have finished his education, be employed, and to have lived independently. She, on the other hand, is likely to have less education, little work experience, and to have moved directly from her parents' home to her husband's. She reaches her adult maturity within the context of the marriage where her growth is influenced by the needs and wishes of her husband and her children. He, generally, reaches maturity as an individual. The two experiences are decidedly different. The emphasis for him is on independence and self-reliance, for her, on sharing and perhaps, sacrificing. His dominance and power in the family is further enhanced by his being the sole or primary breadwinner with the power and prestige that that brings with it in our society. Even if the wife works, she can seldom make as much money as her husband and always has her family responsibilities considered paramount.[4]

And that leads to the second idea which we were discussing, that the two sexes are expected to do different work. Women's work is defined in terms of child rearing and nurturance and men's in terms of protection and occupation. Mainly, the work of adult males is supposed to consist of earning a living and supporting a family. (Later, we will discuss how the pressures to do this have a number of detrimental effects on men.) However, as hard as this may be for some, for most, it enhances and perpetuates male power and prestige in relation to women. The main work of adult women is very different from that of men. It revolves around pleasing, serving, and assisting men and children, tasks which eventuate in a state of dependency, passivity, and powerlessness. How? Well, in many subtle and not so subtle ways.

In a recent article, Barbara Stevens states that in our society, the roles of wife and mother require the subjugation of oneself to the needs of others. This deprives a woman of her identity in a very basic way. These roles are essentially passive in that they require the subjugation of one's own needs to the needs of one's husband and children. "But," says Stevens, "the concept of identity requires the assertion of that identity. No self can survive for long if it never stands up, if it never occupies space."[5]

The loss of identity is exaggerated by other factors as well. In a recent article, Margaret Polatnick makes the point that the nurturing and caretaking tasks of wife and mother often overlap. The role of wife in our society carries with it the expectation that the woman provide for her husband the same services and support, the same ministrations to everyday need, that mothers are expected to provide for children. "Mothering" behavior is indeed not very different from "feminine" behavior. In fact, as many family therapists must have observed in their work, children and fathers often compete for similar services from mother.[6]

Subjugation of oneself to the needs of others and its accompanying restrictions on independence and assertiveness are less obvious for women in the pre-child bearing years of marriage. Several research studies have indicated that with the arrival of children, however, woman's assertiveness decreases, and her dependency and passivity increase. The larger the number of children, the greater the loss of both psychological independence and actual power in the marriage vis-a-vis her husband. This situation is at its height during the pre-school period when child rearing responsibilities are most consuming and economic dependence upon the husband is most extreme.[7]

Add to this the burden of housework. Because the female work role is clearly linked to domesticity, child rearing, and homemaking, it is to the woman that the demands and responsibility for housework are allocated. Despite their intelligence, their talents, and their education, the great majority of American women end up with the sole or major responsibility for keeping the family home clean. The American sex role ideology leads even those Americans who agree that a black skin should not uniquely qualify its owner for janitorial or domestic service to assume that the possession of a uterus uniquely qualifies its owner for precisely such service. In *The Future of Marriage*, Jessie Bernard suggests that the mindless, boring, repetitive responsibilities of housework are making the American woman ill, mentally ill, that is, and Bernard musters an impressive array of studies and statistics to support that view.[8]

Although, if we were to make a tally sheet, men would probably turn out to seem advantaged by our sex role ideology, they by no means escape being handicapped by it also. Robert Seidenberg, a psychiatrist who wrote the book *Marriage Between Equals*, makes just that point. He says:

> . . . it is quite probable that men become victims of their own advantages. An unearned superiority is thrust upon them. This places a constant burden of proof upon them which causes distortions of character and personality which are tragic to behold. The man is placed, often through no personal need or desire of his own, in a position of proving why he, of two people, should automatically be the standard bearer for the family.

> . . . it is the male who is forced consistently to show and prove himself, leading to the hang-ups of eternal competition and inevitable oneupsmanship.[9]

Men are continually measuring themselves against others as well as against their own past achievements. They are loaded with responsibilities to provide, to protect, to succeed. In addition, they are discouraged from developing certain desirable traits such as sensitivity and tenderness. They are discouraged from releasing pent up emotions by crying or otherwise showing emotion. Just as women are discouraged from expressing assertive needs, men are discouraged from expressing dependent needs.[10] Whole people, of course, have both sets of needs. No wonder the physical health of middle-aged men is so much worse than that of middle-aged women, and no wonder that their life expectancy is so much shorter.

In addition to inhibiting the lives of individuals, our restrictive sex role ideology often contributes to less than adequate family relationships. How often has it occurred that when fathers wish to have a close relationship with their children, mothers have successfully kept them in a marginal position? There is no doubt that the need to do this stems from the woman's attempt to safeguard the primary importance of the mother-child relationship. For within our sex role structure, that relationship is crucial to justifying the woman's identity, her indispensibility. She is limited in her access to success on any other grounds.

In a 1971 article in the *American Journal of Orthopsychiatry*, Jean Baker Miller and Ira Mothner make the point that mutually enhancing interaction is not possible between unequals. The authors' vivid descriptions of covert family struggles, fought secretly, often viciously, but with no real understanding of the real enemy and certainly with no victors, but all victims, illustrate their point.

To quote the article:[11]

> Within many homes in which the woman seemed to accept her place as subordinate, one variant or another of the following scenario unfolds. The wife would complain of or even merely mention the family's lacks, the limitations of their budget, the possessions they did not have, the vacations they did not take. She made clear, perhaps without even verbalizing it, her feelings that her husband was less able, less successful, less adequate than other men. She constantly demonstrated his relative unimportance within the home and indicated that his failure to find sufficient time for his family was the result of his own inefficiency. Meanwhile, she flaunted her own qualities as a worker, dramatizing the speed and efficiency with which she cared for the home. She, of course, spent much more time

with the family and used the time to demonstrate her greater devotion and "love." She capitalized upon whatever weaknesses her husband possessed. He tended to make impulsive decisions which he, himself, sometimes regretted. He could never admit this, because his wife magnified these errors, falsely creating the impression that they were the cause of many of the family's problems. By contrasting her own more sober reflections she attempted to establish her superiority. Her husband was unable to defend himself against much of this psychological sabotage. Each charge contained some truth. In family discussions, the wife used his weaknesses to humiliate him and treat him with contempt. In time, he came to feel increasingly inadequate, less successful, less "manly," humiliated and demeaned. His children then regarded him as weak, less masterful and mature than their mother. They turned increasingly to mother for fulfillment of their needs, and simultaneously hated and distrusted her for the destruction of their father.

The wife had waged a devastatingly effective covert campaign, destroying the nominal enemy but gaining no victory. Her husband's effectiveness had been diminished both within the home and outside it. The wife, however, had won nothing. She could not replace the husband she had rendered impotent. She was truly afraid to go out into the world and accomplish anything herself. Indeed, she was ill-prepared and afraid to do so, having earlier surrendered her opportunities for education or work experience in order to advance her husband's. During the course of the campaign, she had also lost much and was made to feel unappreciated as a person and less of a woman.

There are numerous variations on this theme and numerous other examples of how our current system of sex role differentiation has long since outlived its usefulness. It has become basically dysfunctional. It now seems to serve only to aggravate family conflict and to prevent both men and women from developing as full and complete human beings.

As a whole, the mental health profession has not yet seen that point. They still tend to support traditional definitions of masculinity and femininity and to support sex-typed definitions of roles and relationships within the family.

Following a Freudian psychoanalytic model, the profession has generally defined women in basically negative terms, as a passive, dependent, unintelligent, inferior, defective creature.[12] Phyllis Chesler's entire book *Women and Madness* supports the conclusion that ". . . most contemporary female and male clinicians, whether they are disciples of a particular psychoanalytic or psychological theory or not, currently share and act upon traditional myths about 'abnormality,' sex-role stereotypes and female inferiority."[13]

Concrete evidence of this has been supplied by recent research not reported in Chesler's book. A survey of the field reported in the April 1975 *American Psychological Association Monitor* concluded that a very large number of therapists was presently fostering traditional sex roles in their work with patients, showing bias in expectations and devaluation of women and maintaining sexist use of psychoanalytic concepts.[14]

To date, the most impressive work in this area was done by Dr. Inge Broverman and her associates at the Worchester State Hospital in Massachusetts, a study that is fast becoming a classic in the field. The researchers wished to determine what assumptions were held by clinical psychologists about the criteria of mental health. They took three matched groups of male and female clinicians and gave each a list of one hundred and twenty-two character traits—unlabeled and printed in random order. Each group was given a different set of instructions. One was told to choose traits which they felt characterized the healthy adult male, another to choose those which characterized the healthy adult female, and the third to choose those which characterized the healthy adult.

The healthy adult male was typified by such traits as aggressive, independent, objective, active, logical, direct, adventurous, decisive, self-confident, ambitious, worldly.

The healthy adult female was typified by such traits as emotional, intuitive, subjective, submissive, home-oriented, gentle, sensitive to others' feelings, expressive, strong need for security and for dependency.

The most striking finding to come out of the study, however, was that the clinically healthy adult and the clinically healthy male were seen by these psychologists as identical.[15]

This study leads to the conclusion that in the mental health profession, a double standard of health exists for men and women. The general standard of health is perceived as the stereotype for men. For a woman to be considered mentally healthy, she must, in effect, behave in ways that no self-respecting male ever would.

There is, indeed, a further painful paradox existing here. If a woman deviates from the sex-typed stereotypes prescribed for her, if she grows more active, aggressive, assertive, ambitious, self-concerned, for example, she is not perceived by the mental health professional as growing healthier. Rather, she is often perceived as sick. In other words, women who enter a therapeutic encounter run the risk of being considered sick if they display the traits of the normal healthy adult. I suspect that this is as true in group and family therapy as it is in individual therapy today.

Sadly, women's inability or lack of desire to adjust to, or be content with, feminine roles and expectations has been considered by some in the mental health profession as a deviation from natural female psychology rather than as a criticism of such roles and expectations. This handicaps men as well as women. For to the extent that one sex is expected to adhere rigidly to gender role prescriptions, so is the other.

Liberation of women, men, girls, boys, and families means each person acting according to his potentials, abilities, and needs rather than according to the prevailing stereotypes about sex roles and appropriate modes of thought and behavior. For the benefit of all, experimentation with role variation and with role interchangeability is needed. It would be most encouraging to see large numbers of men free to express emotions and to cry, pressuring themselves less to perform or to succeed. It would be most encouraging to see large numbers of women with a greater degree of assertiveness and feelings of competence, pressuring themselves less to subjugate self to familial needs. In terms of work tasks, it would be encouraging to see husbands feeling freer to undertake child care and housework and to see wives freer to undertake careers outside the home.

Harry F. Harlow, who devoted a great portion of his professional life to the study of the critical aspects of infant nurturing, has concluded that "the American male is physically endowed with all the really essential equipment to compete with the American female on equal terms in . . . the rearing of infants."[16] Men can be as effective child carers as women. The same is, of course, true of house care as well.

And women can be as successful as men have been at careers outside the home. This is especially true if they do not conform in other ways to the female sex role stereotype. For passivity, dependence, and nurturance are not highly valued on the job market. Half of all American women eighteen to sixty-four years of age are paid workers. It is, once again, a reflection of the limitations of our gender stereotypes that the greater majority of these working women have paid jobs but not careers.

A career, by its very nature, includes a high degree of personal commitment, a continual striving toward skill and experience development, and at least, a sharing of priorities with one's familial obligations. In our society, careers have been frowned upon for women partially because women's family responsibilities have been considered their primary obligations not to be competed with by any other activities and partially because it has been felt that the husband's position as main breadwinner, and head of the household, and his image of himself as a man would be threatened by his wife's participation on a career level in the world of work. The most recent research in this area seems to indicate that that is not the case. It is not the case, however, for what could be considered the wrong reasons. In a study of fifty-three dual career families, Neal Garland found that in the vast majority of cases, the wife's career commitment was seen by both as clearly secondary to her husband's career and to the wife's domestic duties. Basically, what happens in these families is that the wife takes on the load of two careers, home and occupation, without gaining the status, power, or freedom which an occupational career affords her husband.[17]

And this is not going to be easy to change. In a recent study of two hundred and forty men, Warren Farrell found that the closer proposed gender role changes came to influencing the home environment, the more the men opposed it. Almost all of the men studied were in favor of the Equal Rights Amendment because few saw it as affecting their personal lives. Fewer favored ending differential school training for girls and boys. It was virtually impossible for the men to accept the idea of giving dolls to their sons—much easier for them to contemplate giving baseball bats to their daughters. Indeed, very few of the studied men favored doing away with traditional gender role allocation when it came to child rearing and housework. In other words, men were in favor of women adopting the traditional male stereotype if they so desired but not for men to adopt the traditional female stereotype.[18] This is understandable in view of the low esteem in which that female role is held in our society and the high esteem in which the male role is held.

The family therapist is in a unique position to help families to break out of this sex role straight jacket by encouraging active experimentation with gender roles. If the family therapist tries to mend family crises by encouraging spouses to accept their sex stereotyped niche as so many mental health professionals have done in the past, it is quite likely that he will aggravate family problems and conflicts rather than help to alleviate them. How much more productive it could be to help male and female family members to express their repressed and denied gender role strivings and to encourage them to experiment freely with behaviors attuned to their particular needs, talents, wishes, and inclinations! Excluding no option as deviant or inappropriate because one is a man or a boy or because one is a woman or a girl. The family therapist will have to be aware constantly of his own stereotypes and inclinations in this regard and take care not to allow them to restrict the families' freedom of choice.

In a recent article, Carol Wesley noted that in order to achieve this, every family member will need support in asserting him or herself within an oppressive status quo. And the family as a whole may need support and guidance in learning to accept each member's new self-awareness and emerging life-style.[19]

But families can change from traditional roles and not break up the marriage or damage the children. Rather, such change can, indeed, enhance their functioning as a family and strengthen their ability to meet the outside world.

FOOTNOTES

1. Janet Saltzman Chafetz, *Masculine/Feminine or Human?* (Illinois, 1974), pp. 35-36.

2. Margaret Mead, *Sex and Temperament in Three Primitive Societies* (New York, 1969). First published in 1935.

3. Sandra L. Bem, "Sex Role Adaptability: One Consequence of Psychological Androgyny," *Journal of Personality and Social Psychology*, Vol. 31, No. 4. (1975), p. 635.

4. Judith Stiehm, *The New York Times*, July 2, 1975 (Op-Ed page).

5. Barbara Stevens, "The Psychotherapist and Women's Liberation," *Social Work*, Vol. 16, No. 3 (July 1971), p. 14.

6. Margaret Polatnick, "Why Men Don't Rear Children: A Power Analysis," in John W. Petras (ed.) *Sex Male, Gender Masculine, Selected Readings in Male Sexuality* (New York, 1975), p. 222.

7. *Ibid.*

8. Jessie Bernard, *The Future of Marriage* (New York, 1973).

9. Robert Seidenberg, *Marriage Between Equals* (New York, 1973), pp. 317-318.

10. See Stevens, *op. cit.*, p. 14.

11. Jean Baker Miller and Ira Mothner, "Psychological Consequences of Sexual Inequality," *American Journal of Orthopsychiatry*, Vol. 41, No. 5 (October, 1971), p. 771.

12. For an excellent feminist refutation of basic Freudian theory regarding female development, see Kate Millet, *Sexual Politics* (New York, 1970), pp. 176-203.

13. Phyllis Chesler, *Women and Madness* (New York, 1972), p. 61.

14. Jules Asher, "Sex Bias Found in Therapy," *APA Monitor*, Vol. 6, No. 4 (April, 1975).

15. Inge K. Braverman, Donald M. Braverman, Frank E. Clarkson, "Sex-Role Stereotypes and Clinical Judgements of Mental Health," *Journal of Consulting and Clinical Psychology*, Vol. 34, No. 1, pp. 1-7.

16. Harry F. Harlow, "The Nature of Love," *The American Psychologist*, Vol. 13 (December, 1958), p. 685.

17. Neal Garland, "The Better Half? The Male in the Dual Professional Family," in Constantina Safilios-Rothschild (ed.), *Toward A Sociology of Women* (Massachusetts, 1972), pp. 199-215.

18. Warren T. Farrell, "Beyond Masculinity: Liberating Men and Their Relationships With Women," in Lucile Duberman (ed.), *Gender and Sex in Society* (New York, 1975), pp. 216-248.

19. Carol Wesley, "The Women's Movement and Psychotherapy," *Social Work* (March 1975), pp. 120-124.